An Encounter that Changes Everything

with the **ONE** Heals our Wounds

Unless otherwise noted all scripture quotations are taken from the New International Version of the Bible. Copyright © 1973, 1978, 1984 by International Bible Society.

ISBN 13 978-0692695005
Printed in the United States of America.

I dedicate this book to my family

who inspire me! I love you!

ACKNOWLEDGMENTS

Words cannot express my gratitude toward Jesus, my Lord and Savior. His unconditional love continues to touch me, and His grace never ends. I thank you, Lord, for your revelation and wisdom.

I am also grateful for my family for tolerating the hours I spent writing this book. You motivate me to be better every day.

Special thanks to Pastor Wendy for believing in me. Your mentoring and friendship are invaluable.

Thanks to my sweet friend Crystal Mancha. Thank you for allowing the creativity of heaven to flow through your hands. Your artistic gift is beyond measure.

My church pastors, thanks for always encouraging me to dream big and to pursue my calling.

Thanks to Ruben Rivera, for the wonderful portrait photo. You did an amazing job!

Nora Benny

CONTENTS

FOREWORD

I've always believed and therefore said, "Salvation costs us nothing, discipleship costs us something, but transformation costs us everything!" How much do we want to be transformed into His Image? Every time you wonder what is going on in your life, the answer will be "I am conforming you to the image of My Son." That is His Word and the work of the Holy Spirit.

In Dr. Nora Benny's book, "An Encounter That Changes Everything", you will be empowered by revelatory insight as well as practical applications of the Word of God and personal testimony on how to walk out your "transformational journey!" Every chapter is eye-opening, thought-provoking, and power-packed as she delves into the layers of the Word of God, breaking down strongholds in the very areas of our lives that the enemy would try to destroy us in.

Each chapter builds upon the last and, in my opinion, culminates in the last one with the very key to our success in living the life God intended for us to live before the foundation of the world…A real, life-giving relationship with the Holy Spirit and how He works in our lives to accomplish what He was sent to do! I pray that you devour and enjoy the truths found in this book as I have!

Wendy Borrego, Executive Pastor
Victory Christian Center, Houston, TX

PREFACE

"Jane" (her real name has been changed) was referred to me for counseling because she was having behavioral difficulties at school. She was argumentative and noncompliant. When she came to my office, she seemed very agitated and did not talk much. We started our conversations about anything but school. Jane began by telling me about her friends and favorite things. Eventually, she opened up and we were able to have discussions about her problems at school. We talked about effective ways she could deal with her anger. One day, Jane told me about her issues at home, especially with her father.

Talking about her family was very cathartic for her, particularly when she learned how her family dysfunction was affecting her behavior. We worked to the place where she could do something about her responses to her environment.

Jane is one of many who have emotional wounds. Her family issues were so deep they came to the surface in the form of aggression at school. Like some of us, she did not realize the root of her behavior. It was not until we started dealing with her family issues that her behavior improved.

I can relate to Jane's story, as I have also dealt with the emotional baggage that comes from family dysfunction. Our negative experiences influence the way we think and act. I have how emotional and psychological wounds can be more devastating than physical ones. I know they need to heal properly, just as a physical wound would.

One day, as I reflected upon a situation, the Holy Spirit showed me that emotional wounds are like an onion, which has many layers. Regarding our emotional bank, each layer represents a memory, an emotion, or an experience. In order to get to the core, these individual layers have to be pulled back and dealt with, one by one.

This book is about how you can start your journey to wholeness and healing. Here, the focus is on how God ministers inner healing as we encounter Him. Although there are various ways to deal with emotional wounds, the best way is when God is the source of healing.

I hope you realize you are not alone. Living a life with a wounded heart would be devastating when it does not heal properly. Jesus died on the cross to restore our relationship with God, so we can be whole again.

Inside this book, I tried to use simple words that most people understand, while writing in a way that is theologically and biblically sound. I pray that you will see the heart of the Father, with the revelation of His love and purpose for your life. I would like to encourage you with this: God is very personal. He meets us right where we are and deals with us according to your needs. He will be with you every step of the way, as you embark on a new life journey. I also pray you experience the supernatural, inner healing power of God, as I share the stories of His people, their personal journeys, and their encounters with Him.

CHAPTER 1

WHAT IS INNER HEALING?

Inner Healing is the process of healing and restoration of broken places of our heart where there is a wound. We need to understand how the mind, spirit, and body are connected to learn more about inner healing. We will briefly address some of these approaches.

Across the centuries, this subject has interested philosophers, novelists, theologians, and scientists. Those who tackle this complex subject tend to produce various explanations based on their own fields of study. I will discuss the connection between mind, spirit, and body from three perspectives: biological, psychological, and theological.

For example, the biological model explores how emotions affect our bodies. It describes the function of each system (including our brain) in our bodies and the connection to our emotions. This approach establishes the origin of emotional disorders from a biological and neuropsychological perspective.[i] Through medical devices, brain activity is observed and measured, as people experience emotional distress.

The psychological perspective tries to define mental health abnormality and pathology. It views a disruption in natural and environmental processes as one of the causes for disorders. It also describes how our thoughts and perceptions impact our emotional responses. A mental health disorder is defined as a clinically significant behavior, psychological syndrome or pattern that significantly affects a person's functioning and therefore, increases the risk of suffering, death, pain, disability or loss of freedom.[ii]

Each of these approaches also provides solutions to address various problems. Treatment focuses on relieving symptoms through medication, therapy, or self-help. However, they cannot treat the spiritual condition of the soul and/or the heart.

Now, from a theological perspective, the spirit contains the soul, which lives in the body. Our mind and emotions interact with our spirit and body. In addition, our sins (attitudes and behaviors against the Word of God) affect our physical, emotional, and spiritual wellbeing because of its consequences. The topic of inner healing was first introduced by the spiritual forerunner, Agnes

Sanford. Agnes was the daughter of a Presbyterian missionary in China. In her book, *The Healing Light,* she describes her firsthand experiences related to the healing power of God. Later on, other ministers, such as John and ministers, such as John and Paula Sandford, further expanded the concept of inner healing, utilizing Agnes Sanford's writings.[iii] Therefore, Inner healing, from a Biblical perspective, introduces Christ as the restorer and healer of our mind and soul. In other words, inner healing is God's restorative process of a person's emotional hurts into wholeness. He restores us and satisfies our lives in a way that nothing else can. The psalmist, David, describes this well in Psalm 103:1-5 (NIV):

> *"Praise the LORD, my soul; all my inmost being, praise his holy name. Praise the LORD, my soul, and forget not all his benefits—who forgives all your sins and heals all your diseases, who redeems your life from the pit and crowns you with love and compassion, who satisfies your desires with good things so that your youth is renewed like the eagle."*

If we look at these verses, we can see a sequence of events. First, God forgives our sins. It is important for us to recognize what is separating us from God. We sin when we turn away from God's Word and principles. I believe rebellion is at the root of sin, but God tells us He loves us so much He will always forgive our sins when we ask. Second, He heals us. David declares, in this Psalm, that God heals all our diseases. He does not say He heals some diseases but establishes that God includes all our diseases (including sickness, disorders, and conditions).

Once our relationship with God is established, He addresses our physical, emotional, and psychological needs. Many people don't believe God is interested in our mental health. If God is not interested, why does He address our thoughts, emotions, and feelings in the scripture? God is all knowing. He is the author of creation and because of the ramifications of Adam's and Eve's disobedience he knows what we need. The Lord knows everything that will ever happen in this world (according to 1 Corinthians 2:10-11).

Finally, God redeems us from the pit. Some Bible translations state God redeems our life from destruction. Restoration is a part of that process; God takes us out of our present condition and restores us to our original state (before we were broken). David understood the redemptive nature of God, a thousand years before Jesus' birth and death. The result of God's restorative process is renewal and fulfillment. Renewal gives us a fresh perspective and enables us to rise above our circumstances and pursue our goals. We don't have to go to this process alone alone because God will be with us all along the way.

WHAT IS GOD SAYING?

1. What is inner healing?

2. How receiving inner healing could be beneficial for your life?

3. What does restoration bring?

CHAPTER 2

WHY IS INNER HEALING NECESSARY?

Let's look at the Scriptures again, to gain more insight.
According to the Bible, God created angelic beings before creating
Adam and Eve. The apostle Paul wrote, "For in him all things
were created: things in heaven and on earth, visible and invisible,
whether thrones or powers or rulers or authorities; all things have
been created through him and for him." Colossians 1:16 (NIV).

The Bible gives us an indication there is a hierarchy and an
order in the spiritual realm. For example, there are references to
Michael, the archangel (Daniel 10:13, Daniel 10:21, Daniel 12:1,
Jude 1:9, and Revelation 12:7). In the original Greek language,
archangel, means "chief of angels." Therefore, we can conclude that
Michael had some type of authority that other angelical beings did
not have. There are other types of angelical beings mentioned; the

seraphim and the cherubim (Genesis 5:25, Exodus25:18, Numbers 7:89, and Isaiah 6:2-6). According to Isaiah, Chapter 6, seraphim angels have six wings and worshipped God by making declarations of His Holiness. On the other hand, a cherub is an angel who appears to guard places. Genesis 3:24 tells us that a cherubim guarded the tree of life. Lucifer (also known as the devil) was a cherub and belongs to the cherubim group. The name, Lucifer, is only mentioned in the King James Version of the Bible. Other translations call him a "morning star." According to Ezekiel 28:14, he was "anointed as a guardian cherub." His task designation was to guard the holy mount of God. While we don't exactly know where the mount of God was located, we can certainly ascertain that Lucifer had an important job. Just like the other angels, he had the ability to make choices. Scripture does not tell us how Lucifer's character changed, but it does give us insight, regarding what happened. Lucifer's hunger for power led him to rebel against his Creator (Isaiah 14). He cultivated the desire to be bigger than God and as a result, God disgraced him and threw him out of heaven. Lucifer did not go alone. He took one third of the angels (Revelation 12:4-9). Consequently, scripture addresses the fallen angels as demons. Lucifer, himself, has several names. He is called Satan, devil, deceiver, and a liar, among others. Lucifer's work did not stop when he was expelled from heaven. As a matter of fact, he is the source of evil on the earth (Job 1:7). Satan is against humanity and is determined to deceive and destroy people.

We can trace the devil's work back to Adam and Eve. In Genesis, Chapter 2, when God created a man and a woman, He gave them authority to rule over the earth. God wanted Adam and Eve to enjoy everything. He also wanted them to live forever. To protect them, God gave them a command. He told Adam and Eve not to eat from the tree of the knowledge of good and evil (Genesis 2:17). I would imagine everything was going well with Adam and Eve, until the devil showed up. The devil appeared to Adam and Eve in the form of a snake. He challenged God's command, by enticing them to eat from the forbidden fruit. The first thing Satan did was to question God's Word by asking, "Did God really say…?" One of Satan's tactics is to devalue God's Word, because he knows if we believe God, he can't gain a hold on us. The first mistake Eve made was to engage with the enemy. She gave Satan a listening ear. He garnered her attention.

The next thing he did was to lie. He contradicted what God said (Genesis 3:1-4). We must know that everything that is different from the Word of God is a lie. Unfortunately, Eve believed Satan and disobeyed God. Not only did she eat the forbidden fruit, but she gave some to Adam, who also ate it. I don't believe they had any idea there would be ramifications to their decision. As a result, the relationship between Adam and Eve and God immediately changed. They were forced to deal with the consequences of their own actions. They were not allowed to stay in the Garden of Eden. They soon had to work hard, to get their needs met.

WE ARE BORN WITH SINFUL TENDENCIES

Just like the angels, Adam and Eve were free to act according to their own will. Their choice to disobey God cost them everything. How many times have our choices caused us heartache? Adam and Eve opened the door for sin to enter the world and to influence their lives. The Bible does not say they were unhappy or scared before they encountered the devil. However, everything changed rapidly when they sinned. The scripture says their eyes were opened. They were thrust into another world. They saw and felt differently:

> *When the woman saw that the fruit of the tree was good for food and pleasing to the eye, and also desirable for gaining wisdom, she took some and ate it. She also gave some to her husband, who was with her, and he ate it. Then the eyes of both of them were opened, and they realized they were naked; so they sewed fig leaves together and made coverings for themselves. Then the man and his wife heard the sound of the LORD God as he was walking in the garden in the cool of the day, and they hid from the LORD God among the trees of the garden. But the LORD God called to the man, "Where are you?" He answered, "I heard you in the garden, and I was afraid because I was naked; so I hid."* Genesis 3:6-10 (NIV).

Not only did they realize they were naked, but they felt the need to cover themselves. Note that they covered themselves, because they did not want God to see them in their present condition. Initially, they did not have to cover themselves because their relationship with God was open and honest. The New Living Translation reads in Genesis 3:7: *"At that moment their eyes were opened, and they suddenly felt shame at their nakedness. So they sewed fig leaves together to cover themselves."* For the first time shame is mentioned in the Bible. Adam's and Eve's disobedience opened the door for all kinds of feelings and emotions (both good and bad).

Emotions are part of who we are, and they have a function. They are signals alerting us about what is going on in our bodies. While positive emotions make us feel good, negative emotions cause us to feel bad or uncomfortable. Emotions are considered neutral; in that they give insight into what else is going on in our lives. They are also part of the process of how we respond to our environment. This is critical, because research shows our environment to be just as important as our genetic makeup. A study from Indiana Purdue University shows that the presence of a genetic defect or an environmental offense and threat can interfere with the normal development of some neuronal populations.[iv] Intense emotions, such as anger and fear, can affect our bodies at the cellular level. For example, a factor such as the appreciation of love, anger, or anxiety can influence and modify the outcome of everyone's DNA (deoxyribonucleic acid) design. It can affect how a cell reads the genetic information of a gene.

Historically, researchers have studied the relationship between sensory stimulation and physical influences in the way we respond to our environment. Now, scholars are expanding the traditional model for behavioral development and are studying the relationship of a person's genes and the environment.[v] The information we receive through our senses is influenced, not only by behavior, but also the connections in our nervous system and the current condition of the neural activity.[vi] In simple terms, changes that are caused by environmental factors affect how our cells read genes, but not the molecular structure of our DNA. This is important because, while the sequence of our DNA remains intact, our emotions and behavior can affect our body at a cellular level. Our cells contain the basic and functional structure of our body. Cells contain many substances, including proteins and nucleic acids.

While this information may be new to us, it is not unknown to God, because He is the master creator of our DNA. Each DNA contains a unique molecular structure. God created our bodies with the capability to experience life. Our emotions are not necessarily the problem. The difficulty lies in the choices we make. If we allow negative emotions to control us, and we can't deal with them properly, we can make wrong choices. For example, we might respond aggressively. The apostle, Paul, wrote, "In your anger do not sin. Do not let the sun go down while you are still angry, and do not give the devil a foothold." Ephesians 4:26-27 NIV. When Paul wrote this letter to the people of Ephesus, he described what a Christian life should look like. He also reminded us that as followers of Christ, our minds should be renewed. Consequently, our behaviors should reflect that. Paul used anger as an example. It is interesting that he did not use a different emotion. Maybe he selected anger because it has the potential to affect us at a deeper level. Although Paul acknowledged anger is an emotion we will experience, his emphasis is on our response. In other words, feeling angry is not really the problem, but how we react when we are angry. When people are controlled by anger, they think and act in a way that they normally would not. This can also be dangerous because we don't realize the impact our behaviors may have on others. When we read the chapters following Genesis 3, we see how Adam's and Eve's choices affected the lives of their family members.

Let's look at how their acts of disobedience to God affected their family, especially their children. Adam and Eve had three children: Cain, Abel, and Seth. Cain was the oldest son. He worked in the land (probably in agriculture), while Abel, who was next in line, was a shepherd. One day, both brothers presented an offering to God. Cain gave God a product from the fruit of the land, while Able gave Him a contribution from his flock. Genesis, Chapter 4, reveals that Cain did not present his best fruit, while Abel presented the best of his flock. As a result, God had more respect and regard for Abel's offering. Cain got very angry because God favored his brother's gift over his. He also became sad and depressed. God talked to Cain about his feelings. He asked, *"Why are you angry?"* Genesis 4:6

(NIV). God wanted Cain to deal with his anger. He did not want the emotions to rule over him. God explained to Cain, *"...but if you do not do what is right, sin is crouching at your door; it desires to have you, but you must rule over it."* Genesis 4:7 (NIV). Cain's attitude was not unknown to God, because He is omniscient (He knows it all). However, he was giving Cain a chance, not only to recognize his emotional state, but to deal with his feelings. It is as if God was saying: *I know you are angry right now, but don't let the anger get a hold on you.* God also offered a solution: Cain needed to calm down, control his anger and do what was right. Then, he would have the ability to clearly think over his choices. This story could have had a different outcome, but Cain let the anger embitter his heart and it turned into hatred. Instead, of recognizing his feelings and asking for help, he allowed the anger to control him and acted on it. Consequently, he did the unthinkable by killing his brother. Cain ignored the warning signals that indicated something was wrong. He did not talk about his anger and deal with it appropriately. His anger got the best of him.

Cain's response was tragic. Although his actions were senseless, they give us a major clue about the condition of his heart. We cannot ignore our emotions, especially when they can impair our ability to think rationally. The Bible says, *"But the things that come out of the mouth come from the heart, and these defile them."* Matthew 15:18 (NIV). Cain's expression of anger points to a deeper issue. Holding onto anger can affect our perception of reality, our relationship with God, and our relationship with others. We might not be able to see things clearly or we see things through different lenses; lenses that are not clear.

Although the Bible does not tell us what else Cain did, we see how his decision affected his whole family for generations. If we look at Cain's descendants, we can also read that other family members had anger issues. Scripture gives us examples of people who allowed their anger to control them and the impact it had on their lives. As a result, they lived an angry and bitter life.

What happened to Cain is still happening today. If we turn to the news, we hear of people who are killing each other due to unresolved heart issues. Many times, the loved ones can look back and recount the warning signs. While there are a few individuals who commit murder and feel no remorse for their actions, the majority of them do. Most people never think they could kill someone. However, things do not happen overnight. Eventually, people do lose control and act out the unthinkable, especially when a situation serves as a trigger for what is really going on in their hearts and minds. This is why it is so important for us to be mindful and aware of our emotions. When we understand the way God made us, not only can we learn new methods of dealing with situations, but we can involve Him in the process.

Our brain was created to handle our responses through our five senses. Once information is gathered, it is filtered through our processing center and sends a signal to our body, which triggers the release of hormones and neurotransmitters throughout our nervous system. As a result, there is a physical response. Sometimes, we feel sick in our stomach, have sweaty palms, or experience an increase in our heart rate. These are some of the body expressions that help us become aware of our emotions in response to our environment. Our brains have neurons that receive the hormones and neurotransmitters that have been released. They will prompt our body to switch "on" and "off" when we feel angry. Research shows that stress and anger can affect the brain's function and its' ability to slow down.[vii] A body that is in a constant state of alert might be unable to process its responses adequately. God knew emotions could negatively impact us and He made a provision for this. The apostle, James, inspired by the Holy Spirit, wrote, *"My dear brothers and sisters, take note of this: Everyone should be quick to listen, slow to speak and slow to become angry, because human anger does not produce the righteousness that God desires."* James 1:19-20 (NIV). Anger has the potential to slow our brain's function to respond appropriately. We should not respond immediately when we feel angry. Responding in anger will produce unrighteous (wicked and unjust) actions. We should take some time to cool off. We can take some deep breaths and walk away from the situation and ask the Holy Spirit for assistance. The Bible tells us God will help if we ask. Hebrews 4:16 (NIV) says, *"Let us then approach God's throne of grace with confidence, so that we may receive mercy and find grace to help us in our time of need."* Grace is God's supernatural power that will enable us to do the right thing. We don't have to stay in a state of anger. Jesus died on the cross for our sins, to make us whole, because it is in His heart to mend the broken hearted.

At the beginning of His ministry, He revealed God's will, when He was teaching in the temple. When Jesus read the scroll, the book of Isaiah, He made a declaration indicating He was the one who the prophet Isaiah talked about. God sent Jesus to bring freedom and to heal the broken hearted (Luke 4:18). We don't have to worry about God not understanding our situation. He is very personal and meets us right where we are.

No matter what we are going through, one thing is for sure: God can help us if we ask, because He knows what it feels like. *"For we do not have a high priest who is unable to empathize with our weaknesses, but we have one who has been tempted in every way, just as we are—yet he did not sin."* Hebrews 4:15 (NIV). Jesus experienced love, anger, and suffering while living on the earth just as we do.

GOD WANTS US TO BE WHOLE

Jesus constantly interacted with a diverse group of people who had different life experiences. He ministered to everyone (the poor, rich, religious, non-religious, etc.). He was very personable. Luke tells us that Jesus started His ministry by fasting for forty days. We don't exactly know what kind of fasting He did, but it was likely with water only fast or a liquid one. During fasting, He was tempted by the devil. Satan appeared to Jesus and asked Him to perform various acts. Jesus conquered the temptation by referring to the Word of God. In each instance, He would quote the scripture.

After He fasted, Jesus returned to Galilee. Then, He visited a synagogue in Nazareth. He was speaking to the multitude, when someone gave Him a scroll. Jesus read and publicly announced that the words spoken by the prophet Isaiah, years before his birth, were about Him. Here are those words:

> *"The Spirit of the Sovereign LORD is on me, because the LORD has anointed me to proclaim good news to the poor. He has sent me to bind up the brokenhearted, to proclaim freedom for the captives and release from darkness for the prisoners, to proclaim the year of the LORD's favor and the day of vengeance of our God, to comfort all who mourn, and provide for those who grieve in Zion—to bestow on them a crown of beauty instead of ashes, the oil of joy instead of mourning, and a garment of praise instead of a spirit of despair. They will be called oaks of righteousness, a planting of the LORD for the display of his splendor."* Isaiah 61:1-3 (NIV).

Jesus' bold declaration amazed the people because some knew Him from birth as the son of Joseph. The man they saw growing up as a child, was claiming to be the Messiah that Isaiah wrote about. Note that the prophet Isaiah declared those words, under God's inspiration, hundreds of years before Jesus' birth! Centuries before, Isaiah's revelation revealed God's heart for His people. His plan has always been to redeem and restore us. Jesus' proclamation helps us understand that God has the power to turn our grief and sadness into joy. He can also heal our hearts. God's healing will bring freedom to our body, mind, and soul from any afflictions, because of His love. He loves us despite our choices and behaviors.

God cares about the condition of our hearts. The story of King David illustrates this as well. When the prophet, Samuel, went to Bethlehem to anoint a king, he was looking primarily at the outward appearance. He went to Jesse's house. Jesse had eight sons. David was the youngest. Some of these men were in King Saul's army and looked very strong. David, on the other hand, was a shepherd. Samuel thought one of David's brothers was going to be the new king because of their looks. Every time he saw one of David's brothers, he approached them to anoint them. But God redirected him each time because He was not looking for someone tall, muscular, and strong. God was looking for someone with a tender and pure heart. God told Samuel, *"Do not consider his appearance or his height, for I have rejected him. The Lord does not look at the things that people look at. People look at the outward appearance, but the Lord looks at the heart."* 1 Samuel 16:7 (NIV).

Why is God so interested in the affairs of our hearts? Because everything comes from our heart: our thoughts, feelings, and emotions. Recently, I had the opportunity to talk to a wealthy person about God's goodness and mercy. Initially, I had a hard time listening, because I had my own ideas about wealth and could not

not understand what this person was talking about. However, I kept hearing God saying to me, "Listen to the heart." After several times, I started paying attention to the person's emotions and feelings. I tuned in my heart toward the Lord, and He gave me specific words and strategies about what to say and do. We prayed and this person felt really blessed. I could have missed the opportunity to be a blessing if I let my opinions and feelings dictate my actions. Here are some additional Scriptures where God addresses the heart.

"Above all else, guard your heart, for everything you do flows from it." Proverbs 4:23 (NIV)

"Anxiety weighs a man down, but a kind word cheers it up." Proverbs 12:25 (NIV)

"Hope deferred makes the heart sick, but a longing fulfilled is a tree of life." Proverbs 13:12 (NIV)

"Each heart knows its own bitterness, and no one else can share its joy." Proverbs 14:10 (NIV)

No one is exempt from trials. Suffering and sorrow are part of the human experience. Therefore, each one of us will face difficult times, at some point, in our lives. Towards the end of His ministry, Jesus talked to His disciples about His departure. He told them the time would come when they would no longer see Him (physically). The disciples could not understand what He was saying when he said, *"...In this world you will have trouble. But take heart! I have overcome the world."* John 16:33 (NIV). Jesus prepared His disciples for what was about to come.

Even Jesus faced trials and tribulations in His life. For instance, He was in distress when He went to Gethsemane to pray, prior to His death. The Bible says, *"Then he said to them, "My soul is overwhelmed with sorrow to the point of death. Stay here and keep watch with me."* Matthew 26:38 (NIV). We need to read the scripture to understand Jesus' sorrow. Earlier, Jesus had dinner with His disciples and uncovered the truth about one of His follower's betrayals. Imagine having dinner with your friends and the Holy Spirit reveals to you that one of them is about to betray you and sell you out.

When you confront your friends, one of them confesses. Not only that, but he has gone behind your back to conspire with your enemy. Jesus knew His death was near. He was inundated with sadness and grief. He knew this was just the beginning of His crucifixion journey. Yet, He carried out God's plan because it was the only way to redemption. Jesus' death was a sacrifice of love and because of His sacrifice, we can have a relationship with God. We can experience His mighty power, which transforms our hearts and minds. This is one of the many reasons why the Bible is still relevant and active for our world today.

As we read the scripture, we discover we can relate to those people who experienced emotional turmoil in their own lives. We see how they overcame. Here some emotional Biblical expressions:

- Nehemiah: *So the king asked me, "why does your face look so sad when you are not ill? This can be nothing but sadness of heart."* Nehemiah 2:2 (NIV)

- Job: *"But when he saw that the three men had nothing more to say, his anger was aroused."* Job 32:5 (NIV)

- David: *"Why, my soul, are you downcast? Why so disturbed within me?* Psalm 42:5 (NIV)

- Jeremiah: *"Oh, my anguish, my anguish! I writhe in pain. Oh, the agony of my heart! My heart pounds within me, I cannot keep silent. For I have heard the sound of the trumpet; I have heard the battle cry."* Jeremiah 4:19 (NIV)

- Naomi: *"Return home, my daughters; I am too old to have another husband. Even if I thought there was still hope for me—even if I had a husband tonight and then gave birth to sons; would you wait until they grew up? Would you remain unmarried for them? No, my daughters. It is more bitter for me than for you, because* the LORD's hand has turned against me!" At this they wept aloud again. Then Orpah kissed her mother-in-law goodbye, but Ruth clung to her." Ruth 1: 12-14 (NIV)

- Hannah: "*In her deep anguish Hannah prayed to the LORD, weeping bitterly. And she made a vow, saying, "LORD Almighty, if you will only look on your servant's misery and remember me, and not forget your servant but give her a son, then I will give him to the LORD for all the days of his life, and no razor will ever be used on his head.*" 1 Samuel 1:10-11 (NIV)

- Paul: "*For I wrote you out of great distress and anguish of heart and with many tears, not to grieve you but to let you know the depth of my love for you.*" 2 Corinthians 2:4 (NIV)

These individuals experienced distress, anguish, sadness, depression, bitterness, or anger. Does this sound familiar? We can relate to so many of them at different points in our lives. Nevertheless, no matter what we are going through, one thing is for certain. God knows how we feel. "*For we do not have a high priest who is unable to empathize with our weaknesses, but we have one who has been tempted in every way, just as we are—yet he did not sin.*" Hebrews 4:15 (NIV). He knows and understands us. God is able to help if we ask, "*For everyone who asks receives; the one who seeks finds; and to the one who knocks, the door will be opened.*" Matthew 7:8 (NIV).

WHAT IS GOD SAYING?

1. How Adam and Eve's choices affected his family for generations?

2. Can you identify a negative pattern in your life that has been in your family line for generations?

3. What does the Bible reveal about God's heart?

CHAPTER 3

HURT BY DECEPTION

In Genesis, Chapter 21, Abraham and Sarah have struggled to have children for years. Abraham succeeded in having a child with one of his servants, requested by Sarah, because she wanted to have children. Both were old in age when God finally told them they were to have a child. Sarah, amazingly, soon became pregnant. She gave birth to a boy, which Abraham named Isaac (means 'laughter'). Isaac grew swiftly and soon it was time for him to get married. He chose Rebekah and loved her dearly. Rebekah was also unable to conceive children, until God answered her prayers. She gave birth to twins: Esau and Jacob. Jacob was the youngest of the twins by birth order. He came out of the womb grasping his brother, Esau's, heal (Genesis 25). According to scripture, Isaac favored Esau, while Rebekah loved Jacob. Esau became a hunter, while Jacob stayed at home. It was customary for the oldest son to receive his father's blessing. This could only be done once because the father had only one birthright blessing to give. Rebekah knew this and she wanted Jacob to receive this blessing, instead of Esau. With the help of his mother, Jacob persuaded Esau to sell him his birthright and tricked his father (who was weak and could no longer see) into blessing him, instead of his brother. When Esau went to see his father, he asked for his blessing, but it was too late. Isaac, then, learned his younger son deceived him. Esau was also very angry, as he realized what he gave up. He planned to wait for his father's death before killing his brother. Rachel learned about Esau's plan and warned Jacob. She asked him to leave to escape his brother's wrath. Fearing his brother's anger, Jacob fled, deciding to seek refuge with his Uncle Laban.

On his way, he chose to stop for a break. Jacob fell asleep and had a dream. He saw a stairway coming down from heaven to earth. He also saw angels ascending and descending on the staircase. In the dream, God spoke a blessing upon Jacob and his children. This was Jacob's first divine encounter with the Lord. God chose to reach out to Jacob, in the form of a dream, and pronounce a blessing, instead of addressing his deceiving ways. God could have declared a consequence for Jacob's dishonesty. Instead, He spoke a blessing. He saw beyond the natural. To men, Jacob was a liar and a dishonest man. He deserved to be punished. But God saw somebody different through His redemptive eyes. The Bible story lets us know that Jacob received those blessings and, eventually was the father of many nations. Jacob was not married when he had his first encounter with God. Yet, God chose to reveal to him what was in store. This event marked the beginning of Jacob's journey towards healing and restoration. It had such a profound effect on Jacob's life that he made a decision to follow God. He proceeded to give an offering to God, as a symbol of his commitment. Wow! What an experience. We can't encounter God and not be transformed.

Jacob became aware of God's presence. He seemed surprised, because he did not think God would reach out to him after all he had done. How many times do we walk through life wounded, not knowing God is closer to us than we think? We fail to understand how a love can be so great that it covers our multitude of sins and wounds.

After the dream, Jacob continues his journey. Up to this point, he has a history of deceit and a promise from God. As Jacob gets to his destination, he first meets Rachel. He falls in love with her immediately. Rachel was the daughter of his Uncle Laban, which she was his cousin. It was common to marry within the family. Jacob meets Rachel, for the first time, and wants to marry her. However, Laban deceives Jacob and gives him Leah, his older daughter. In the father's eyes, he needed to have Leah marry first. Now, the tables are turned against Jacob. His uncle tells him that he will give Rachel in marriage if Jacob works for him for seven years.

It might have seemed that his life was getting worse. He had an amazing experience with God. He received a promise and now, he is the one being deceived. Jacob deceived his brother, and his uncle tricked him. Even though God gave Jacob a promise, he still reaped the consequences of his actions. Sometimes, we have to face the results of our behavior in the natural sequence of events. But, neither God, nor His plan for us ever changes (Numbers 23:19). He did not change his plan for Jacob either.

Jacob marries Rachel after seven years of work. Then, he decides to stay with his uncle and work for him another seven years. Jacob's business prospered. His family grew until he determined it was time for him and his loved ones to have their own place. Jacob tells his uncle about his plan. Laban's attitude towards Jacob changed for the worse. He tried to trick him again, but this time he failed.

Jacob flees from Laban. He heads back home. Jacob takes his family and possessions. However, he still has unresolved issues with his brother, Esau. As we read, we can see how Jacob's character is changing. He is determined to mend his relationship with his brother and to make things right. After so many years of separation, Jacob wants to meet with his brother. Jacob prepared his family and servants for this encounter. He also brought gifts. On the way, Jacob decides to spend the night in the camp. There, he has another encounter with God. Jacob wrestled with a man (who was an angel) and asked him for a blessing. Jacob told the man he was not going to let him go until he received this blessing. The man asks Jacob for his name. Then, he said to Jacob: *"your name will no longer be Jacob, but Israel, because you have struggled with God and with men and have overcome."* Genesis 32:28 (NIV). What a statement! We see God's redemptive nature through Jacob's experience. Jacob is on his way to mend a broken relationship and he encounters God on the way. Previously, we have seen a man whose heart has been wounded by deception and now, we see a different person.

Jacob is someone who made a commitment to serve God and wants to do the right thing. His actions reflect the healing and transformation taking place in his heart. The beginning of Jacob's healing started with his first encounter with God (in the dream). Now, Jacob is no longer a deceiver, but a new person in God.

People who are hurt by deception might believe they are something different than they really are. Their reality becomes distorted, and their actions reflect that. That is not what God sees. When He looks at us, He sees us for who He created us to be. God is truth. He wants us to know the truth because He desires us to be free. John 8:12-34 shows that, on more than one occasion, Jesus revealed Who He was to the people He encountered. He also took time to teach and share His heart with those who believed in Him. Jesus affirmed them and encouraged them to follow His teaching, as His disciples. He said to them: *"Then, you will know the truth and the truth will set you free."* John 8:32 (NIV). God wants for His people to know who we are in Him. He says we are His children. Because He is our Father, we are a royal priesthood. 1 Peter 2:9 (NIV) It does not matter what other people think or say about us. God's thoughts are what really matters. Because of this, Jacob's name was changed. He was no longer a deceiver, but a transformed person. Now, his new name reflected his new identity.

This is not the first time God changes somebody's name in scripture. Why is that? The answer is simple: because He loves us. *"...And I pray that you, being rooted and established in love, may have power, together with all the saints, to grasp how wide and long and high and deep is the love of Christ."* Ephesians 3:17-18 (NIV).

WHAT IS GOD SAYING?

1. Writing in a journal or notebook is an effective tool to use for the healing process. It also helps clarify your feelings and emotions.

2. Have you been affected by deception? List at least one area of your life in which you have felt deceived (example: people, relationships, work, finances, etc.).

3. How has this experience affected your perception of the situation?

4. What God says about you and the situation? Write down any thoughts that come to your mind. One of the ways God speaks to us is through our thoughts, like a still small voice.

5. Ask God to help you forgive yourself or those who have deceived you.

CHAPTER 4

HURT BY A DYSFUNCTIONAL FAMILY

Jacob rejoined his family in the land of Canaan. He had children with four women. There were twelve children in all. The Book of Genesis tells us Joseph was the eleventh of Jacob's twelve sons and Rachel's firstborn. Can you imagine what it would be like living in a family of that size? Although having big families was common in Biblical culture, these days, in our culture, most families are relatively smaller. Just as Jacob's mother favored him, Jacob favored Joseph. Even though Jacob served God, he was still human and made mistakes. The Bible tells us that Jacob loved Joseph more than the rest of his children. In showing his love, he gave Joseph a fancy coat.

The gift presentation did not set well with his siblings, who were already jealous and hated him. Jacob had probably done other things, in favor of Joseph, that he did not do for his other sons. To make matters worse, Joseph told his brothers about two dreams, in which he had envisioned them bowing down in deference to him. Joseph's brothers hated him even more. While no family is perfect, Jacob's family was extremely dysfunctional.

A family is considered severely dysfunctional when its members exhibit behaviors that are deemed outside the norm. These behaviors have a severe negative impact on the entire family. In other words, dysfunction impairs a family's ability to function adequately. Many times, these behaviors are symptoms of deeper problems. People who live in severe dysfunction may assume differing roles, depending on family dynamics and positions. Family Constellation is such a construct. According to the theory, each child assumes a position. Each position comes with some particular characteristics.[viii] For example, the older child tends to be the overachiever and a leader. The middle child strives in competition, while the younger sibling is babied or spoiled. These dynamics can cause resentment in the family system. Such was the case in Jacob and Rebekah's family. They had to deal with the challenges that came from favoritism and anger.

Often, children who live in unhealthy family systems are not always aware of the family dynamics. They think the behaviors they see, and experience are normal. Typically, the family does not talk in terms of patterns, but more in terms of isolated events or facts[ix].

Although the Bible does not give us insight into Jacob's children's thoughts, it is obvious that Joseph's brothers were very resentful. They watched their father giving their younger sibling a gift, when they received nothing. In their eyes, they were not important to Jacob.

In addition, an unhealthy family is typically labeled either "enmeshed" or "disengaged." The characteristics of enmeshed behaviors involve an emotional intensity and reciprocal dependency, while disengaged behaviors share a remarkable absence of emotional intensity in family attachments[x]. We cannot confuse enmeshing behaviors with closeness. A family that has good boundaries and is closed is also healthy. This was not the case in Jacob's family. His family exhibited disengaging behaviors.

Joseph was about seventeen years old when his brothers' jealousy took a turn for the worse. The situation grew to a point where his brothers were actively planning to get rid of him. They did not want him to be part of the family any longer. In the meantime, Jacob sent Joseph to spy on his brothers, as they took the sheep to pasture. He asked Joseph to check on them and report back. Joseph easily found his brothers. When they saw him approaching, they considered killing him. However, not everyone was on board with this idea. Reuben, the oldest brother, convinced the other brothers to throw Joseph in a dry well instead, because he felt the need to protect his younger brother. Here, we see the oldest child leading the rest of the children. He apparently had some measure of authority over them, as they agreed. They put Joseph into the dry well, took his coat off and left him there. No doubt, Joseph felt betrayed and lost. How could his brothers do something like this?

The brothers hung around the well until they saw an oncoming caravan of merchants. Suddenly, Judah, one of the middle children, had another idea: to sell his brother as a slave. He probably saw his brother as a competing force for their fathers' love and determined to fix the situation permanently. Perhaps he believed that someone could get Joseph out of the well and his father would find out what they had perpetrated. We don't know. Nevertheless, he convinced his brothers to sell Joseph as a slave. Reuben was not there when this sale took place. Joseph was sold, for almost nothing, to Midianite traders. What a mess!

Let's think for a moment about what just happened. Nine out of eleven brothers decided to sell a younger brother because they despised him. Joseph's life just changed completely, in a matter of seconds. Reuben returns to check on Joseph, only to find he was not in the well. Reuben feels anger and sorrow. He does not know what do to. It is his brothers who come up with a plan to explain Joseph's disappearance to his father. They knew he would be devastated. A story like this would have been on the front page of our newspaper.

All the brothers agreed to lie to cover themselves. They killed a goat and put its blood on Joseph's coat. They told his father he was killed by a wild animal. Jacob's heart was broken and full of grief. Jacob continued to show a similar dysfunctional family pattern. With Joseph gone, Jacob was determined to protect his youngest son, Benjamin, born from his relationship with Rachel.

This family would definitively be a good case for therapy. In dealing with their issues, they failed recognize how the transactions and decisions being made were influenced by extended family networks. For example, Jacob was his mother's favorite. Now he has favorites. Jacob's mother lied to her husband, because she wanted Jacob to receive his blessing instead of Esau. Similarly, Jacob's uncle lied because he wanted his older daughter to get married first.

Jacob's children lied to him. We can trace these patterns of behaviors to prior generations. If we went backwards, we could see a pattern of people disengaged from one another. They lied and committed murder, because of jealousy.

Remember the story of Cain and Abel? They had another brother, Seth. His history is tied to Abraham (Jacob's grandfather) several generations before. There were serious strongholds in this family that were very difficult to break. How could God use a situation like this to bring healing into Joseph's life and his family? How could these strongholds be broken?

In the natural, it seems impossible that a loving God would allow such horrible things to happen to a young person. If He is a good God, how could Joseph go through all he did? While we don't understand everything concerning God and His sovereignty, we can still know that He is God. We also need to remember He created us with the ability to make choices. Each one of these individuals made decisions on their own. Their fate was the result of their own sinful desires and decisions. Nonetheless, our decisions do not change Who God is or His plans for us:

"For I know the plans I have for you," declares the Lord, declares the Lord, "plans to prosper you and not to harm you, plans to give you hope and a future." Jeremiah 29:11 NIV)

"You are good, and what you do is good; teach me your decrees." Psalm 119:68 (NIV)

"But God demonstrates his own love for us in this: while we were still sinners, Christ died for us." Romans 5:8 (NIV)

Since God is good, where does evil come from? As we learned in Chapter 2, the enemy is the source of evil and he is constantly trying to destroy us. He is *"like a roaring lion looking for someone to devour."* (1Peter 5:8). Even though Joseph's family was falling apart, God still had a plan for him and he prospered in everything he did. An event having the potential to totally destroy Joseph, became the channel for further prosperity. We could not have seen this by judging his future, based on what happened to him, because we never have the whole picture. This is why the apostle, Paul, said *"in all things God works for the good of those who love him, who have been called according to His purpose."* Romans 8:28 (NIV).

Let's continue looking into Joseph's journey. The merchants sold Joseph to Potiphar, who was Pharaoh's Official in charge of the Palace Guard. Joseph initially did well in Potiphar's house, however, there was still more calamity to come. The Official's wife framed him (because she wanted to have sex with him, and Joseph refused). Joseph ended up in jail. At this point, Joseph was still going through trials. His whole life seems like a mess. However, even in Jail, Joseph was kind and helped others. God gave him the gift of interpreting people's dreams. The interpretations caused Joseph to gain credibility among his prison mates. Eventually, Pharaoh heard about his reputation and ability. Joseph was called to interpret two dreams for Pharaoh, after other people had tried unsuccessfully. Pharaoh's dreams contained information about the future: seven years of prosperity and seven years of famine (shortage of food). Joseph not only interpreted the dream, but also gave the king a solution to deal with the famine. As a result, Pharaoh made him governor over Egypt.

What a great story! Egypt experienced prosperity in the land, which Joseph managed, by storing food for the next seven years. When the famine came, the people of Egypt were prepared. People came from other countries to buy food. Joseph's family was no exception. His brothers traveled to Egypt to purchase supplies. When they saw Joseph, they did not recognize him, but he knew his family. Genesis 42 reveals it was not easy for Joseph to contain his emotions concerning his brothers. The Bible tells us he cried several times, before he revealed himself to them. When Joseph identified himself, they were speechless. He cried so loud other people around the palace could hear him (Genesis 45:2). The brothers stood silent at first, but Joseph chose to forgive them. They wept together and reconciled with him. Eventually, the brothers brought their father to see Joseph.

This is a great example of forgiveness and reconciliation. It shows us that God goes beyond family dysfunction and generational patterns. Joseph was able to break away from a history dating back to Abraham. He could have deceived his brothers or taken revenge by killing them. His life could have had a horrible ending full of anger, bitterness, and revenge. Instead, his relationship with his family was mended and the entire family received healing.

God was always working in Joseph's life, behind the scenes, to prepare him for that decisive moment when he needed to make a healing decision. Joseph did not know what would eventually happen and the healing process did not take place overnight. The story of his family covers many chapters in the Bible; Genesis 37 through 50. About Joseph, the Bible says God was with him several times. He was with him when he was in Potiphar's house, the prison, and Pharaoh's palace. Joseph was thirty years old when he became governor of Egypt. Thirteen years passed; from the time he was sold by his brothers. Joseph acknowledged his relationship with God was the cathartic force in bringing healing to his family. Joseph married and had two sons: Manasseh and Ephraim. Joseph had two reasons for naming his boys: "Because God has made me forget all my trouble and all my father's household" and "because God has made me fruitful in the land of my suffering." (Genesis 41:51-52). Joseph had an outstanding revelation. He knew the supernatural power of

God helped him survive the things he went through and enabled him to forgive his family.

Joseph dealt with his emotional baggage before forgiving his family. But, once he forgave, the restoration of the family unit began. Reconciliation and healing took place.

WHAT IS GOD SAYING?

1. Has anyone committed an offense against you or were you an offender?

   a. If you were offended, you can make a choice. If you decide to forgive, you can write a letter of forgiveness to the person (offender). You don't have to give it to them. You can destroy it afterwards.

2. Say a prayer. As you talk to God, you might tell Him, "God I forgive _____ and release him/her to you. From this day forward, I will not hold him or her accountable for what he or she did or carry the burden of their offense. Amen."

3. Take a moment, as God's overwhelming peace flows into your life.

4. If you were the offender, ask God for forgiveness and forgive yourself. You might want to ask the person for forgiveness, either in person or through a letter. Keep in mind that forgiveness is for your freedom. It is not conditioned upon the person's response.

CHAPTER 5

HURT BY FEAR AND DEPRESSION

We don't know a lot of personal information about Elijah, other than the knowledge that he was a Tishbite from the region of Gilead. Elijah is one of the major prophets of the Old Testament, during the reign of King Ahab (9th century BC). A prophet is someone inspired by God. Prophets deliver God's message to His people, concerning either the present or the future. Not only did Elijah speak on behalf of God, but he demonstrated God's power with signs and wonders.

At the time of Elijah, the land was divided into two kingdoms: the kingdom of Israel (north) and the kingdom of Judah (south). King Ahab reigned in the north. We read in 1 Kings,

Chapter 17, that Elijah delivered a message from the Lord to King Ahab concerning an impending famine. Two years later, when Elijah returns to speak to the King for a second time, the Lord sent the message He was about to send rain.

Initially, Elijah meets with Obadiah, one of Ahab's officers, who was a devout man and loved God. In his past, Obadiah helped one hundred prophets, by hiding them and giving them food when Jezebel (the king's wife) tried to kill them. Ahab was not happy and became angry. His wife was persecuting God's prophets, causing a lot of chaos. Elijah insisted on confronting Ahab because he was serving other gods. He proposed to gather all the people of Israel and the prophets of Baal (their god) to prove the true God. Elijah spoke with boldness when he challenged the king's prophets. He asked them to build an altar to sacrifice animals upon. After its construction, he asked the four hundred and fifty prophets of Baal to have their gods burn the offering. The prophets asked, but nothing happened. They shouted and danced, but nothing still happened. They cut themselves with swords and spears, as part of their ritual. The altar remained the same.

When it was Elijah's turn, he put twelve stones and added water to the altar. Then, he prayed to God. Fire from heaven consumed the water and burned up the offering, the altar, the stones, and even the soil. What a demonstration of the power of God! Elijah trusted God. He knew He would respond to his prayer. When the people of Israel witnessed the event, they fell on their faces. They recognized God, as their Lord, by saying, "The Lord, he is the God." (I Kings 18:39).

Elijah ordered the execution of the false prophets. The people killed them. Nobody escaped. Afterwards, the rain God previously announced for the land came. The king went home and told his wife about God's display. She became enraged at the fate of her priests of Baal and threatened Elijah. She sent a messenger to let him know she would kill him the very next day. Elijah was full of fear. He ran away. The irony! After a supernatural demonstration of God's power, Elijah allowed one person to intimidate him.

Elijah fled with his servant. But later, he left him at Beersheba and went alone into the wilderness. He sat down under a tree and prayed that he might die. Elijah told God: *"I have had enough, Lord. Take my life as I am no better than my ancestors."* (1 Kings 19:4). Elijah fell asleep-feeling angry, tired, and exhausted. Suddenly, he had a divine encounter. An angel of God appeared to him. The Bible says the angel touched him and talked to him at the same time, Elijah experienced not only a visitation, but a physical touch from God. Notice, at this point, Elijah was physically nourished because the angel fed him. He gave him bread cooked over coal and water. God sent an angel to spend time with Elijah. Angels are His messengers. Elijah ate, but he was too exhausted, so he went back to sleep. The angel returned to wake him. He asks him to eat more food and tells him that he has a long journey ahead. God took care of Elijah's physical need first. Elijah felt stronger and was ready to embark on his journey to the Mountain of God. He walked for forty days and nights. When he arrived at the mountain, he crawled into a cave and went to sleep again. God visited Elijah again, talking with him while he was in the cave. The Lord met the prophet, while he was in the cave. God was willing to meet him where he was. He did not ask him to come out of the cave first. God knew Elijah was struggling. God next addressed his emotional need. Elijah was lonely and scared. Subsequently, God asked Elijah what he was doing. All Elijah saw was the bad in his situation. Elijah told God, "The people of Israel have abandoned your covenant, destroyed the places of worship and murdered your prophets. I'm the only one left, and now they're trying to kill me." (1 Kings 19:10). Notice he did not talk about his supernatural experience while in the presence of the king and his prophets. He was still feeling hopeless. Elijah is depressed and in despair.

It is not surprising to read Elijah's response. We know the power that negative words have over our body. Negative thoughts release stress producing hormones and neurotransmitters that interrupt the normal functioning of the brain.[xi] Negative thoughts can also impair logic, reason, language processing, and communication.

When we vocalize our fears, different regions of our brain are activated.[xii] In fact, negative words, spoken in anger, have a greater impact. They deliver alarm messages throughout the brain, interfering with the decision-making process and a person's ability to act in a rational manner.[xiii]

God takes our mental condition seriously. Depression is a psychological disorder that affects a person's thoughts, feelings, and actions. Research shows major life stressors are risk factors for depression. Slavish and Irwin (2014) investigated the neural and physical responses associated with environmental stress. They proposed that experiences linked to social threat and adversity regulates the part of the immune system that regulates inflammation and therefore elicit a biological response.[xiv] In other words, a main factor of this response, can elicit profound changes in behavior (including sad mood, anhedonia, fatigue, psychomotor retardation, and social-behavioral withdrawal). There are many factors that could have contributed to Elijah's condition: the stress of having to deal with the king, physical exhaustion, and the pressure of dealing with the people of Israel. We must not rule out the king's wife's threat. Elijah's fear paralyzed him.

God instructed Elijah to leave the cave, go to the mountain and wait until He passed by. The act of getting out of the cave was symbolic because Elijah did not feel like doing it. Elijah became part of his own healing process by taking action. I firmly believe God intended him to participate in the process all along.

Finally, God addressed his spiritual need. There is a healing that comes only from being in the presence of God. Elijah's condition needed serious attention, because of the complexity of his situation. He was surrounded by so many challenges. God wanted to restore hope. Elijah's body was physically exhausted, his mind was troubled, and his spirit was broken. The Bible tells us things happen when we spend time in His presence. As Elijah waited on God, he felt a powerful wind. Then, an earthquake. After the earthquake, fire came. With each presentation, Elijah thought God was presenting himself in strong and mighty ways. However, the prophet did not find Him there. Instead, God showed up in a gentle whisper.

Elijah finally recognized God's presence. He put his cloak on his face and stood. Elijah's condition was so delicate that the Lord addressed him in a gentle manner. He showed up in a way that was unexpected. Sometimes, we form our own ideas of how God should heal us and expect Him to do so but we should open our heart and mind to receive God's healing His way. Elijah covered his face when He found God in the gentle whisper. When the Creator of the universe shows, it will elicit a response. We cannot encounter God without a transformation.

Elijah, even standing in the presence of the Holy one, is still focusing on the circumstances, instead of His God. But God was not done with Elijah. He encouraged Elijah. He told him about the seven thousand people that were still in Israel, who did not bow down to the idols. Elijah could not see what God was doing because he had lost hope. When we lose hope, our view of life becomes skewed and obscure. Our sight takes on a dark manner. In other words, we adopt a negative attitude. Our thoughts and emotions are out of alignment. We tend to see our problems and circumstances as bigger than they really are. We start believing our situation will never change. Sometimes, we act just like Elijah did. Even though he was in the presence of God, his mindset needed restoration.

God rebuilt Elijah's physical health, healed his broken heart, and restored his mind by speaking the truth. Elijah's healing did not happen overnight. God healed him through a series of divine encounters. In the end, he was no longer depressed. Elijah cried out to God, and He responded. Notice, as part of the healing, the Lord needed to address Elijah's perceptions of Him. How many times have we tried to define God? We feel we know Him, based on our experiences, and formulate ideas on how the Lord should treat us. But God showed Elijah another attribute, which is as powerful as any other. When we are in God's presence, things start to change, and healing comes. In His presence there is freedom, deliverance, joy, and everything we need.

> *Because you will not abandon me to the realm of the dead, nor will you let your faithful one see decay. You make known to me the path of life; you will fill me with joy in your presence, with eternal pleasures at your right hand* Psalm 16:10-11 (NIV).

> *Surely you have granted him unending blessings and made him glad with the joy of your presence* Psalm 21:6 (NIV).

> *Hear, LORD, and be merciful to me; LORD, be my help. You turned my wailing into dancing; you removed my sackcloth and clothed me with joy, that my heart may sing your praises and not be*

silent. LORD my God, I will praise you forever
Psalm 30:10-12 (NIV).

Elijah's story represents the present condition of many of us today. We are stuck and feeling hopeless. We don't believe God will understand what we are going through. The truth is, we can come to Him with confidence. We can find rest in His presence: *"Let us then approach God's throne of grace with confidence, so that we may receive mercy and find grace to help us in our time of need."* Hebrews 4:16 (NIV). God knows how we feel. We live in a society that focuses largely on works, but the final work was already done on the cross when Jesus died. We don't have to go through life dealing with things on our own. He paid the price, so we can enjoy life abundantly.

> *Therefore Jesus said again, "Very truly I tell you,*
> *I am the gate for the sheep. All who have come*
> *before me are thieves and robbers, but the sheep*
> *have not listened to them. I am the gate; whoever*
> *enters through me will be saved. They will come in*
> *and go out, and find pasture. The thief comes only*
> *to steal and kill and destroy; I have come that*
> *they may have life, and have it to the fullest."*
> John 10:7-10 (NIV).

WHAT IS GOD SAYING?

1. List one situation that is overwhelming for you right now. Write down how this situation makes you feel.

2. Select a quiet place where you can spend a few minutes with God. Look for scripture that speaks to your situation. For example, if you are feeling hopeless, grab a Bible and find the verses that talk about hope. You can also go online and find free online Bible software to search for key words.[xv] Write down those scriptures and meditate (focus on it for a long time) until you feel God's peace in this area.

3. Ask God, "What is a lie I believe about You?" Write it down. Then, ask Him: "What is the truth?" Write it down.

4. Encourage yourself in the Lord. Think about the last time you focused on a challenge you had and how God helped you through it. If He helped you once, He would do it again!

5. Do not isolate yourself. Seek out help. You don't have to do this alone. We were created to worship God and to have fellowship with one another.

CHAPTER 6

HURT BY LUST

We can learn about David in 1 Samuel, Chapter 16. David's father, Jesse, was from Bethlehem. The Bible does not give us the name of his mother. Jesse and his wife had eight children. David was the youngest. He was healthy and good looking. David's early occupation was to attend his father's sheep as a shepherd. He also played music.

During this time, Saul was the King of Israel. His time as King was nearing an end when the Lord asked Samuel (one of Israel's prophets) to anoint a successor. Jesse presented seven of his eight sons to Samuel, but none of them met His qualifications. Eventually, Jesse brought in David. God told Samuel David would be the next King. Also, during this time, King Saul was tormented by an evil spirit. When David played his harp, the King would experience peace. Scripture tells us God's favor was upon David. Saul also liked him very much. However, his opinion of David changed as his popularity among the Israelites increased, particularly after he killed Goliath (a champion Philistine and enemy of Israel and Judah). Saul became jealous of David. He persecuted him and wanted to kill him. David knew how Saul felt. He had the opportunity to harm Saul but refused to act upon it because he understood authority and knew the King was still God's appointed leader.

Years later, David was anointed as King (after Saul's death). David was thirty years old when he became King. He reined for forty years. 2 Samuel 5:4 (NIV). David accomplished many things, including conquering the city of Jerusalem and bringing back the ark to that city. He also had some failures. In 2 Samuel, Chapter 11, we can read about one of his major setbacks.

One day, David was walking around the roof of his palace, when he saw Bathsheba, a beautiful woman, taking a shower. Lust entered David's heart. He wanted to know more about her, so he sent someone to find out who she was. David learned she was married to a man named Uriah. A married woman should be off limits in any time frame. But, not for David. He started pursuing her. Although he knew a relationship with her would result in adultery, he continued forward with his plan. Eventually, David had a sexual relationship Bathsheba, and she became pregnant. When Bathsheba told David, he devised a scheme to kill her husband. He sent Uriah to the war and asked one of his men to leave him alone, so he could be killed. Uriah went to battle, and David's plot worked. Uriah was killed. When Bathsheba heard the news, she was upset and grieved over his death. What a sad story. David the king and a worshiper of God, was being led astray by lust. He did not have to give in to temptation when he saw Uriah's wife. David's behavior continued to spiral out of control. He married Bathsheba and she gave birth to a baby boy. Because God loves us such much, He continues to reach out to us, even when we are deep in sin. God sent a prophet named Nathan to speak with David about what happened (2 Samuel 12:9). Initially, David did not understand Nathan's words. But when he realized he had sinned against God, his heart was broken. Although God forgave him, David had to face the consequences of his sin. His child died. David was full of grief. In Psalm 51, David pleads for forgiveness and asks God to cleanse his heart.

Have mercy on me, O God, according to your unfailing love; according to your great compassion blot out my transgressions. Wash away all my iniquity and cleanse me from my sin. For I know my transgressions, and my sin is always before me. Against you, you only, have I sinned and done what is evil in your sight; so you are right in your verdict and justified when you judge. Surely I was sinful at birth, sinful from the time my mother conceived me. Yet you desired faithfulness even in the womb; you taught me wisdom in that secret place. Cleanse me with hyssop, and I will be clean; wash me, and I will be whiter than snow. Let me hear joy and gladness; let the bones you have crushed rejoice. Hide your face from my sins and blot out all my iniquity. Create in me a pure heart, O God, and renew a steadfast spirit within me. Do not cast me from your presence or take your Holy Spirit from me. Restore to me the joy of your salvation and grant me a willing spirit, to sustain me. Then I will teach transgressors your ways, so that sinners will turn back to you. Deliver me from the guilt of bloodshed, O God, you who are God my Savior, and my tongue will sing of your righteousness. Open my lips, Lord, and my mouth

*will declare your praise. You do not delight in
sacrifice, or I would bring it; you do not take
pleasure in burnt offerings. My sacrifice, O God,
is a broken spirit a broken and contrite heart you,
God, will not despise. May it please you to
prosper Zion, to build up the walls of Jerusalem?
Then you will delight in the sacrifices of the
righteous in burnt offerings offered whole; then
bulls will be offered on your altar.* Psalm 51
(NIV).

David's sins brought on devastation into his life. He realized
he hurt himself, others, and most of all, God; he needed healing and
restoration. His pain was so great the Bible says even his body
ached. Although David committed a great offense against God, he
constantly reflected upon God's goodness and repented of his sins.
Because of his relationship with God, the Bible describes David as a
"man after his own heart." (1 Samuel 13:14).

We might not realize it, but when we sin against God it will
affect our relationship with Him. Just like David, we might feel
miserable and remorseful. Interestingly, it took David some time
before he repented. He did not initiate the reconciliation process. The
Lord had to send someone to talk to him. But when he understood,
he cried out to God and repented. The Lord responded because He is
love.

*For as high as the heavens are above the earth, so
great is his love for those who fear him, as far as*

the east is from the west, so far has he removed
our transgressions from us. As a father has
compassion on his children, so the LORD *has*
compassion on those who fear him." Psalm
103:11-13 (NIV)

David put himself in the situation. He did not have to go after a married woman, yet he yielded to the temptation. James tells us that *"but each person is tempted when they are dragged away by their own evil desire and enticed. Then, after desire has conceived, it gives birth to sin; and sin, when it is full-grown, gives birth to death."* James 1:14-15 (NIV). The devil is the one who brings temptation. Because he knows our weaknesses, he will try to tempt us in those areas. If we don't act quickly, we find ourselves giving in to sin. Then, we must deal with the consequences. Sin brings nothing but hurt, bondage, and pain. Thank the Lord for His goodness and mercy.

God reached out to David and forgave his transgressions when he repented. In Hebrew, the word transgression is *"pasha"* which means "rebellion." Even when we rebel against God, He still forgives us. God does not remember our past mistakes but sees us through His divine lenses.

WHAT IS GOD SAYING?

1. Identify an area of your life where you are being tempted.

2. Read 1 Corinthians 10:11-13. How is God speaking to you?

3. How can you resist temptation? Write at least three ways you can resist your personal enticements.

4. Ask God to search your heart and to unveil any area that needs restoration and healing. Be willing to repent and ask God for forgiveness.

5. Find a person with which you can be accountable to pray and who will help you stay on track.

CHAPTER 7

HURT BY SHAME

Scripture notates several divine encounters certain women had with God. Our next story will always stand out, because of the circumstances surrounding her. We find this woman in John, Chapter 8. The Bible does not give us her name, but we know she was a troubled woman with a lot of issues. She was caught having an affair with a married man, by the teachers of the law and the Pharisees. According to the laws of the Old Testament, people who committed specific offenses (including adultery) were stoned to death. Normally, this would have taken place outside the camp or the city (Leviticus 24:14). On this day, the punishment was occurring near Jesus, on the Mount of Olives. According to law, both the man and the woman who commit adultery were to be killed. Interestingly, they only brought forth the woman, and not the man, who was just as guilty as she was.

We can only imagine the shame this woman must have felt. Not only were her actions detestable, but she got caught. Picture her in front of Jesus, surrounded by a multitude. The Pharisees dragged her in and made her stand up, while they told Jesus, and everyone else, what she has done.

Shame is a powerful and painful emotion linked to many moral and social dilemmas. It has the potential to affect an individual's identity and self-concept.[xvi] When people feel shame about themselves, they feel exposed, worthless, and powerless. From a psychological perspective, shame is also associated with depressive disorders.[xvii]

Jesus did not say much when the Pharisees brought the woman to Him. He simply bent down and wrote something in the dirt. Next, He stood up, looked at the crowd and said, *"Let any one of you who is without sin be the first to throw a stone at her."* John 8:7 (NIV). In other words, Jesus asked them to throw a stone only if they were not guilty of any sin. One by one, people left the premises, probably speechless and offended. Suddenly, the woman was standing in front of Jesus without any accusers. She was face-to-face with the Son of God!

Jesus asked *"Woman, where are they? Has no one condemned you?"* As she looked around and did not see anyone, Jesus further said, *"Then neither do I condemn you. Go now and leave your life of sin."* (John 8:10-11). Let's pause here for a moment. According to the law, this woman deserved the death penalty. Although the religious people had a reason to bring her to Jesus, they had no case against her, because their own hearts were wicked. They did not actually care about the law. Otherwise, they should have brought the man as well. They only wanted to see if Jesus would break the law. Instead, they were confronted with their own wickedness.

Jesus asked the woman to turn her life around. He forgave her. In other words, He asked her to repent. Repentance requires us to turn around and change our actions. This was a turning point in this woman's life. She started with a traumatic experience and was facing the death penalty. She ended up forgiven and free.

Jesus' actions reflect the heart of a compassionate God, while the actions of the religious people mirror what the devil does. He is the accuser. He wants people to fall into sin. Once they fall into sin, he constantly reminds them of their failures. This is how the enemy works. First, he brings the temptation and patiently waits for us to yield. Then, he accuses us once we sin. James 1:14-15 (NIV) says, *"But each person is tempted when they are dragged away by their own evil desire and enticed. Then, after desire has conceived, it gives birth to sin; and sin, when it is full-grown, gives birth to death."* The consequence of sin is spiritual death. Without God, our destiny has no life. This woman's destiny was about to end. Instead, she received forgiveness and healing. This story is relevant because Christ shows us, why He came. He entered the world to save and heal the sinners and not to condemn them. Jesus wanted to bring this woman to repentance, by showing her His compassion and mercy. He also showed mercy for the accusers by revealing them their sins. As a result, she received a new life. She had an experience she will never forget.

WHAT IS GOD SAYING?

1. Are you carrying a shame connected to an offense? If yes, what is the offense?

2. Look at the following scripture: Luke 4:14-19; John 3:16; Romans 5:16; Romans 10:9-10.

3. Write down what God is speaking to you through these verses.

4. The Bible says, "*those who look to him are radiant; their faces are never covered with shame.*" Psalm 35:5 (NIV). Ask God to show you how He feels about you.

CHAPTER 8

HURT BY SELF-RIGHTEOUSNESS

Formerly known as Simon, Peter was the son of Jonah (Matthew 16:17). He lived in Bethsaida and had a brother named Andrew. Peter's personality was characterized by his fervor, energy, and impulsivity. He became one of the first followers of Jesus.

On one occasion, God gave Peter a revelation of the Messiah. Jesus was in the villages of Caesarea Philippi with his disciples when He asked them who they thought he was. Peter had an astonishing revelation! He said, *"You are the Christ, the Son of the Living God."* (Matthew 16:16). Even though the disciples walked with Jesus, none of them could answer Jesus' question. Peter could, but only because it was revealed to him.

Peter can be considered one of Jesus' close friends. Jesus took Peter and two other disciples with Him when He needed to pray before his crucifixion (Matthew 17). He had a relationship with God. He witnessed the transfiguration when Elijah and Moses appeared and conversed with Jesus high upon a mountain (Mark 9:2-8). Jesus commissioned Peter to shepherd his flock (John 21:16-17). Peter was so close to Jesus, he even tried to defend Him when the soldiers came to arrest Him (John 18:10-11).

Peter also had a special moment with Jesus. According to John, Chapter 21, Jesus was eating with His disciples, when He asked Peter if he loved Him. Peter said, *"Yes, Lord, you know that I love you."* Jesus then asked Peter again. It is no coincidence that Jesus asked Peter a third time. In this passage, the Greek word, ἀγαπᾷς means "agapa" which comes from agape love.[xviii] Agape is love as ultimate and final. In other words, Jesus asked Peter, "Do you love me with a self-sacrificing love?" Each time Peter said "yes" to Jesus. Then, Jesus asked him to feed his sheep. Just like a shepherd care for his sheep and will do anything for them, Peter was to care for people with a sacrificial love (John 21:18-19).

Peter's life was not always filled with amazing experiences. At times, he did not say or do the right thing. Matthew, Chapter 26, reveals some of the events that took place in Jesus' life prior to His crucifixion. He shared those with Peter. In one particular incident, Jesus was eating with His disciples when He revealed that one of them would betray Him. Judas revealed his true motives and everyone was in shock. After their meal, all went to a place called the Mount of Olives, where Jesus tried to prepare His disciples for His coming death. He also told them He was going to rise from the death and return to Galilee. Then, Jesus predicted Peter's denial. When Peter heard Jesus, he told Him *"Even if all fall away on account of you. I never will."* Matthew 26: 33(NIV). Peter did not understand His Master's revelation. He wanted to let Him know he would be there for Him. As a good friend, Peter had honorable intentions, but God knew his heart. Jesus told Peter he would deny Him three times. Peter was offended by Jesus' prediction. He believed he would never deny Him. How many times do we act is if we know more than God? We think we know better and forget Who He is. Sometimes, we can act like we are more righteous than everyone else. Peter was no exception.

As Jesus predicted, He was arrested, and Peter denied Him three times. Not only did he deny Him; but he also swore an oath. The Bible tells us after the third time, Peter wept. Can you imagine how Peter must have felt? He witnessed his Savior and friend taken away to be crucified and could not stand by Him. Like some of us, Peter fell short. He had a self-righteous attitude that led him to believe his actions were worth something. In fact, he was offended when Jesus told him what was about to happen. Peter did not think it was possible. Self-righteousness is one of the ways the devil deceives people. We are deceived when we shift our attention to ourselves and focus on our own abilities. Our actions might seem good and Godly, but God sees us for who we are. *"All a person's ways seem pure to them, but motives are weighed by the LORD."* Proverbs 16:2 (NIV).

Peter sobbed, when he realized what had happened. This moment was significant. He learned from his experience and moved on. After all, God did not hold his mistakes against him. When God touches us, our hearts are restored. Surrendering our hearts causes us to fall in love with Him. Peter was never the same; he was forever changed. According to the book of Acts, Chapter 2, Peter was praying with others when he was filled with the Holy Spirit. In other words, God poured out His Spirit and power over him. Peter stood up with the other disciples and spoke to the crowd with boldness about Jesus. This time, he was not embarrassed. On that day, about three thousand people were moved by his message and asked Jesus to be the Lord of their lives. What an amazing transformation! Peter began his ministry journey. He talked to others about God, healed the sick, and was even sent to prison. Peter gave his life (agape love) in the name of the Lord. He was crucified, his head facing down. Peter's story is a testimony of love. He encountered the Son of God in a personal way, despite his failures. Peter accomplished amazing things for the Kingdom of God.

WHAT IS GOD SAYING?

1. Do you consider yourself self-sufficient? If so, in which area (s)?

2. Find a quiet place and ask the Lord: What would You like me to do about the things You just showed me?

3. Ask yourself this question, "Am I willing to give God this area of my life and allow Him to work in me?"

4. Read John 15:5, *"I am the vine; you are the branches. If you remain in me and I in you, you will bear much fruit; apart from me you can do nothing."* Meditate on this Word and ask God for insight. Afterwards, write down what this verse means to you.

CHAPTER 9

HURT BY RELIGION

Formerly known as Saul, Paul was from the tribe of Benjamin. His family was from Tarsus (Acts 9:11). We don't have any information about his mother, but we know that Paul had a sister (Acts 23:16) and other relatives mentioned in the Bible (Romans 16:7).

Paul was born a Jew. He grew up in the city. Paul was educated, under the law, as a Pharisee (Philippians 3:5). His father was also a Pharisee (Acts 23:6). The Pharisees were a sect who taught Mosaic Law (found in the Old Testament) and its traditions. Pharisees were extremely religious. They attempted to uphold strict precepts and rules that were impossible to follow (Matthew 15:2-6). The Pharisees had a hard time with Jesus and His message because they wanted him to follow their rules (which they could not even follow themselves).

Paul was also very religious. He was educated under Gamaliel (a very prominent Rabbi) and was zealous about the traditions and religious law. Paul was very passionate about what he thought to be God's work (Acts 22:3-4). Because he believed Jesus was not the Messiah, he went to the Jewish high priest and asked for a letter giving him the authority to arrest people who followed Him (Acts 9:2). Paul actively persecuted the followers of Christ and sought their deaths. Paul was also present during the death of Stephen (Acts 22:20). Stephen was a Jew who accepted Jesus as his Lord. He was full of faith and God's spirit. God moved through him with signs and wonders. The religious people did not like Stephen because he was proclaiming Jesus as the Son of God. People were leaving their previous religions to follow Christ. So, they arrested him. Stephen was stoned to death. The witnesses put their coats at Paul's feet (Acts 7:57). After Stephen's death, *"Saul began to destroy the church. Going from house to house, he dragged off both men and women and put them in prison."* Acts 8:30 (NIV).

Paul thought he was doing the right thing. He believed Christians (the followers of Jesus) were a religious and political threat. God had a different plan for Paul. Acts 9:1-19 describes Paul's personal experience with God on his way to Damascus. He was carrying warrants to persecute and arrest more Christians. Suddenly, he saw a bright light and fell to the ground. Paul heard a voice that said: *"Saul, Saul, why do you persecute me?* Acts

9:4(NIV). For the first time, Paul heard the voice of the One he thought he was working for. This is what religion does to people. It emphasizes works, instead of relationship. When Paul heard God's voice, he recognized it was different. There was something about the Voice that spoke with authority. Paul thought he knew about God but did not know Him. Paul asked, *"Who are you, Lord?"* God responded, *"I am Jesus, whom you are persecuting."* Acts 9:5(NIV). Imagine spending your entire life learning about God. You believe you know Him. You are working for Him. Then you realize, the whole time, you were working against Him. Paul is encountering God, Himself, for the first time in his life. Paul had his experience with God after Jesus was raised from death. God wanted Paul to know he was persecuting Jesus, the Son of God. Paul was probably in shock when he learned he was doing wrong in God's name. He had good intentions but was too focused on the law.

Many people with good hearts and intentions have fallen into the trap of religion. Religion, without a relationship with Jesus, is in vain. Like Paul, people do the same things over and over, in the Name of Jesus. They want to reach God through their own actions. It is possible to know a lot about God and still not know Him. Individuals who know a lot about God rely on their own knowledge. They have an answer for everything, but there is no fruit in their lives. They get disappointed and hurt because they work hard and see no results. Consequently, they become angry because they don't understand true love. If only the Pharisees and the Sadducees would have seen Him for who He was! They could have had God and gone to heaven without relying on themselves. They were blinded by their own ideas and beliefs about God. Their beliefs caused them to live a life of guilt and judgment, because they could not live up to religious expectations. It is only through Christ that we are restored and made whole.

Paul was originally bound by religion. However, his encounter with God was the beginning of his relationship with Jesus. He started walking into the destiny that the living God had for him. When the spirit of religion is broken, our heart and spirit is open to receive what God has for us. Our eyes and ears are adjusted. It is an awesome experience. Paul's transformation had such an impact that many found Jesus through him.

Paul was not the only one who misunderstood things about God. There were times when even the disciples did not understand God. For instance, on one occasion, they asked Jesus: *"What we must do to do the works God requires?"* (John 6:28). The disciples were looking for requirements, but Jesus' answer was simple. He told them, *"The work of God is this: to believe in the one who he has sent."* (John 6:29). In other words, you don't need to perform in order to know God; you just need to believe. God wants us to believe in Jesus, who died on the cross and rose from the dead and is the Son of God. It was God's love and desire for humanity that moved Him to give up His Son, Jesus. What a beautiful picture of unconditional love.

Jesus went to heaven after His resurrection (Acts 1:9). His disciples were sad and did not know what was going to happen next.

However, God did not forget about His people. He made provision and sent the Holy Spirit to guide, comfort and empower believers (Acts 1:8). The Holy Spirit guides us to Christ. In the next chapter, we will discuss the person of the Holy Spirit.

WHAT IS GOD SAYING?

1. Do you feel you can't live up to God's expectations? If so, write down the things you do to please God?

2. Ask God to help you identify the lies you believe about Him.

3. Read the following scriptures: John 3:16, Ephesians 2:8-9, John 6:28-29.

4. Write down what God is speaking to you through scripture.

CHAPTER 10

THE WONDERFUL WORKS OF
THE HOLY SPIRIT

This chapter was the hardest for me to write. I wrestled with the fact that I am not a theologian, by any means. How could I write about such an important Person? Then, I heard a sweet voice in my Spirit that encouraged me to write from the Word of God, my heart, and from my experiences with Him.

The apostle, Paul, wrote a letter to the people who lived in Philippi. In this letter, he discussed certain issues of Christian living, such as dealing with worry and lack. He also encouraged believers to get rid of emotional baggage by addressing the mind (Philippians 4:1-23). Paul emphasizes the importance of having a renewed mind (with new attitudes). It is very important that our minds be brought into harmony with the mind of God, as He desires for us to walk in total restoration. He knows when we are hurting or broken, as emotional wounds can also be devastating. Hebrews 12:1(NIV) tell us, *"Therefore, since we are surrounded by such a great cloud of witnesses, let us throw off everything that hinders and the sin that so easily entangles. And let us run with perseverance the race marked out for us."* As Christians, we have the hope of eternal life, however, we will go through the challenges of our existence while we are in this world. In spite of this, God wants us to enjoy our days to the fullest.

WHO IS THE HOLY SPIRIT?

Recently, my husband and I visited my sister-in-law's church in Waxahachie, Texas. That day, there was such a sweet Presence of God. During worship, the Holy Spirit started ministering to me. Suddenly, as I worshiped, I saw pictures of different scenarios in my life. Some of the memories were painful and traumatic. I felt overwhelmed by the mental pictures and how I was feeling. Immediately, I heard the Holy Spirit saying to me, in a small, still Voice: *"I got your back."*

I felt such a peace and a love I can't explain. A few minutes later, the Holy Spirit told me He was there to heal people's hearts at the point where the soul and the Spirit meet. God wants to heal the hearts of His people. While there is nothing wrong with seeking human help; there are areas of our hearts that can only be healed and transformed by the power of the Holy Spirit. I have spoken with people who feel they know everything about God. They always have an explanation. Often, they limit God with their human understanding. By no means, am I trying to do this by writing this Chapter. I know God is bigger. He is such a loving God. He loves us and wants to interact with us. There are so many things He wants to show us. There is so much of Him we don't know. His arms are open. His heart is for you and me because He wants us to walk whole and in victory. Jeremiah 29:11 says that God has a plan for us, and it is GOOD. He wants to give us hope, because when we lose our hope in Him, we lose everything. I don't know what you are going through but know there is ONE Who knows all about it and is willing to help you. *"Now to him who is able to do immeasurably more than all we ask or imagine, according to his power that is at work within us, to him be glory in the church and in Christ Jesus throughout all generations, forever and ever! Amen."* Ephesians 3:20 (NIV).

When we look at the scripture, we learn the Holy Spirit is the Third person of the Trinity. He was present when the world was formed. Genesis 1:2 tells us that *"the Spirit of God was hovering over the earth."* The Holy Spirit has existed with God since the beginning of any existence. He was a part of the creation process (Genesis 1:26). He is not an "it", but a Person with His own attributes. In the New Testament, Jesus introduced the Holy Spirit to His disciples when He prepared them for His death. Jesus told them:

"All this I have spoken while still with you. But the Helper (Comforter, Advocate, Intercessor—Counselor, Strengthener, Standby), the Holy Spirit, whom the Father will send in my name [in My place, to represent Me and act on My behalf], He will teach you all things. And He will help you remember everything that I have told you." John 14:25-26 (AMP). Jesus refers to the fact that the Holy Spirit was also sent by God. The Father, the Son, and the Holy Spirit are always in agreement. The Holy Spirit was sent, not only to comfort us, but to bring the Word of God, His knowledge and revelation. He is God with us. We must look at what the Bible to learn what it says about Him:

- The Holy Spirit always reveals the heart of God. *"The Spirit of the Sovereign LORD is on me, because the LORD has anointed me to proclaim good news to the poor. He has sent me to bind up the brokenhearted, to proclaim freedom for the captives and release from darkness for the prisoners, to proclaim the year of the LORD's favor and the day of vengeance of our God, to comfort all who mourn, and provide for those who grieve in Zion, to bestow on them a crown of beauty instead of ashes, the oil of joy instead of mourning, and a garment of praise instead of a spirit of despair. They will be called oaks of righteousness, a planting of the LORD for the display of his splendor."* Isaiah 61:1-3 (NIV) What a beautiful picture. In this passage, the Holy Spirit is referred to as the Spirit of the Lord. This was common terminology in the Old Testament. He is also called the Spirit of God. God's heart has always been for the poor, the broken, and the captive. What an amazing God we serve!

- The Holy Spirit has feelings. *"And do not grieve the Holy Spirit of God, with whom you were sealed for the day of redemption."* Ephesians 4:30 (NIV). In the English dictionary, the word "grieve" means: causing someone to feel sad or unhappy; feeling or showing grief or sadness. In Isaiah 63:10, the people of Israel grieved the Holy Spirit with their attitudes and actions. Our actions can cause the Holy Spirit to feel sad. In fact, in 1 Thessalonians 5:19, Paul warned the Thessalonians not to *"*quench*"* the Holy Spirit. In other words, he encouraged the believers not to leave the Holy Spirit out from their everyday lives. The Holy Spirit wants to be involved with us daily.

- The Holy Spirit supports us. *"But very truly I tell you, it is for your good that I am going away. Unless I go away, the Advocate will not come to you; but if I go, I will send him to you."* John 16:7 (NIV). When the Holy Spirit speaks, He does it in our favor. He is available 24/7 every day of our lives, ready to assist us.

- The Holy Spirit comforts us. John 14:26 (AMP). The Holy Spirit helps us when we are worried or afraid. How does He comfort us? By reminding us of God's promises.

- The Holy Spirit helps us to pray. Romans 8:26 (NIV) says, *in the same way, the Spirit helps us in our weakness. We do not know what we ought to pray for, but the Spirit himself intercedes for us through wordless groans.* As we pray, the Holy Spirit leads us. There are times when we might not feel like talking to God, but the Holy Spirit intervenes for us, with sounds we cannot understand.

- The Holy Spirit is powerful. *"But you will receive power when the Holy Spirit comes on you; and you will be my witnesses in Jerusalem, and in all Judea and Samaria, and to the ends of the earth."* Acts 1:8 (NIV). God's power has no limits. We have access to the same power that raised Jesus from the dead. Romans 8:11 (NIV) says, *"And if the Spirit of him who raised Jesus from the dead is living in you, he who raised Christ from the dead will also give life to your mortal bodies because of his Spirit who lives in you."* We can walk in the same authority Jesus walked in while He was on the earth. God says that we will see miracles, signs, and wonders because of His power.

- The Holy Spirit is our teacher. *"For the Holy Spirit will teach you at that time what you should say."* Luke 12:12 (NIV). He helps us understand the Bible, how it applies to our situation, and how we can apply it. The Holy Spirit will give us the insight (the revelation) we need.

- The Holy Spirit brings conviction. *"But very truly I tell you, it is for your good that I am going away. Unless I go away, the Advocate will not come to you; but if I go, I will send him to you. When he comes, he will prove the world to be in the wrong about sin and righteousness and judgment: about sin, because people do not believe in me."* John 16:7-9(NIV). An advocate is someone who publicly supports and aids someone in their cause. Jesus says the Holy Spirit is for us. He wants us to do well. He will convict us of wrongdoing, so we can turn around and change.

- The Holy Spirit speaks truth. What a better person to tell us the truth! John 16:13 (NIV), says, *"But when he, the Spirit of truth, comes, he will guide you into all the truth. He will not speak on his own; he will speak only what he hears, and he will tell you what is yet to come."* The truth, will set us free. John 8:32 (NIV).

- The Holy Spirit inspires us. 2 Timothy 3:16 (NIV) tell us that *"All Scripture is God-breathed and is useful for teaching, rebuking, correcting and training in righteousness, so that the servant of God may be thoroughly equipped for every good work."* The Holy Spirit inspired the prophets to speak to His people *"For prophecy never had its origin in the human will, but prophets, though human, spoke from God as they were carried along by the Holy Spirit."* 2 Peter 1:21 (NIV).

WHO IS LEADING YOU?

Recently, I had to prepare a sermon for one of my Bible classes. I spoke about wisdom. As I studied for it, the Lord revealed to me the differences between being led by human intellect and being led by the Holy Spirit. The following table illustrates it well:

HUMAN INTELLECT	HOLY SPIRIT
Relies on the mental capacity; reasoning that comes from human nature, experience, and knowledge.	His knowledge comes from God and His Word.
Looks at different alternatives when facing challenges.	Gives us the best alternative.
Helps us to know facts about God.	Helps us to know God.
Seeks explanation.	Gives us revelation.
Leads us away from God.	Leads us to God.
Glorifies man.	Glorifies God.

When we are led by the Holy Spirit, our lives change, and we glorify God. In Acts, Chapter 2, the disciples, who were praying with others, received a visitation from the Holy Spirit. When this happened, they started speaking in other tongues. Peter explained the Holy Spirit to the crowd. This is the same person who denied Jesus, before His crucifixion, speaking boldly about the Holy Spirit. After Peter's message, three thousand people repented of their sins and started a new relationship with God. They also grew in their knowledge of God. The Bible says that *"They devoted themselves to the apostles' teaching and to fellowship, to the breaking of bread and to prayer. Everyone was filled with awe at the many wonders and signs performed by the apostles. All the believers were together and had everything in common."* Acts 42-44 (NIV). When you have a relationship with the Holy Spirit, you get to know God. Your devotion towards Him increases; but you also develop healthy relationships with others.

A RELATIONSHIP WITH THE HOLY SPIRIT

How can you have a relationship with the Holy Spirit? The first thing we need to know is the relationship starts when we surrender our lives to Jesus and ask Him to be the Lord of our hearts and life. Jesus came to this earth and died for sins, so we could have relationship with God and eternal life. John 3:16 (AMP) says God loved us so much He sent Jesus, His Son, to die for us, so we could enjoy life eternall*y. For God so [greatly] loved and dearly prized the world, that He [even] gave His [One and] only begotten Son, so* *that whoever believes and trusts in Him [as Savior] shall not perish, but have eternal life.* Jesus is the only way to God. In John, Chapter 14, Thomas asked Jesus how he could know the way to God. *Jesus answered," I am the way and the truth and the life. No one comes to the Father except through me."* John 14:6 (NIV). Jesus' answer was simple. No one can know God without having a relationship with Jesus.

The second thing we need to know is the Holy Spirit comes and lives in our life when we commit ourselves to follow Jesus. 1 Corinthians 3:16 (AMP) tells us: *Do you not know and understand that you [the church] are the temple of God, and that the Spirit of God dwells [permanently] in you [collectively and individually]?* The Holy Spirit knows everything about us, even prior to our birth. On one occasion, God spoke to the prophet, Jeremiah, and told him: *"Before I formed you in the womb I knew you, before you were born I set you apart; I appointed you as a prophet to the nations."* Jeremiah 1:5 (NIV). Some scholars believe Jeremiah was a young teenager when God spoke to him. He was so overwhelmed by this experience that he could not see what God was saying to him. But God does not look at how we see ourselves, but how He sees us in Him. He knows every detail of our lives and our utmost deepest secrets. He even knows things we don't know about ourselves. When we fellowship with God, the Holy Spirit will reveal to us unknown things.

WALKING WITH THE HOLY SPIRIT

We have established the foundation of the existence of the Holy Spirit throughout scripture, from the Old Testament and through the New Testament. Let's look at what happens when the Holy Spirit moves in our lives:

- We declare God's will. In Numbers, Chapter 11, we can read the story of Israelites who were complaining. Moses, their leader, spoke to God. He asked God for direction, as the situation had gotten so bad, he did not know what do to. God told Moses to gather seventy elders to help him. He was going to send the Holy Spirit (who was in Moses) to rest upon the elders as well. This is what happened: *"when the Spirit rested upon them, they prophesied [sounding forth the praises of God and declaring His will]. Then they did so no more."* Numbers 11:25 (NIV). When the Holy Spirit moves in us, we declare God's wonderful works.

- We receive wisdom. *"Now Joshua son of Nun was filled with the spirit of wisdom because Moses had laid his hands on him. So the Israelites listened to him and did what the LORD had commanded Moses."* (Deuteronomy 34:9 (NIV). Who does not want to receive Godly wisdom? One of the key elements of receiving wisdom is reverence. If we position ourselves in an attitude of honor and respect towards the Holy Spirit, He will give us wisdom. Wisdom goes beyond human understanding. It enables us to make decisions, based upon Godly principles.

- We do things we cannot do in the natural.
  "The Spirit of the LORD came powerfully upon him so that he tore the lion apart with his bare hands as he might have torn a young goat. But he told neither his father nor his mother what he had done." Judges 14:6 (NIV). Samson came from a mother who was barren and childless. The Bible says God gave him supernatural strength, as he was destined to deliver the Israelites from the Philistines. When the Holy Spirit came upon Samson, he killed a lion with his bare hands. In the natural, it would be impossible for anyone to kill a lion without using an object. In the same way, when the Spirit moves, we can do impossible things because our God is powerful.

- We are changed. *"The Spirit of the LORD will come powerfully upon you, and you will prophesy with them; and you will be changed into a different person."* 1 Samuel 10:6 (NIV). When Samuel, the prophet, anointed Saul to be the King of Israel, he told him he would be a different person when the Holy Spirit came upon him. Indeed, Saul's life changed when the Holy Spirit touched him. The people who saw Saul, after his encounter with the Holy Spirit, knew something was different. Saul began to prophesy. He had boldness and the passion to declare God's greatness. We cannot encounter the Holy Spirit and not be affected. As He transforms our hearts, we become more like Christ: we think, feel, and act differently than before. We become a new person in God.

- We receive instructions. *"He gave him the plans of all that the Spirit hadputinhismindfor the courts of the temple of the LORD and all the surrounding rooms, for the treasuries of the temple of God and for the treasuries for the dedicated things."* 1 Chronicles 28:12 (NIV). King David wanted to build a house for God. The Holy Spirit gave him specific construction instructions. He also told David his son, Solomon, was the person chosen for the assignment. We are confident in knowing the Holy Spirit will guide us in what we ought to do.

- We are convicted. *"Then the Spirit of God came on Zechariah son of Jehoiada the priest. He stood before the people and said, "This is what God says: 'Why do you disobey the LORD's commands? You will not prosper. Because you have forsaken the LORD, he has forsaken you'."* 2 Chronicles 24:20 (NIV). During this time, the people of Judah turned away from God. When the Holy Spirit came upon the priest, he brought conviction and judgment upon his people.

- We are purified through the fire. *"The Lord will wash away the filth of the women of Zion; he will cleanse the bloodstains from Jerusalem by a spirit of judgment and a spirit of fire."* Isaiah 4:4 (NIV). As we get closer to God,

His light will shine on us and expose any impurities or sins. The Holy Spirit is the agent of our sanctification. His fire cleanses and refines us.

- We have visions. *Then the Spirit lifted me up, and I heard a great rushing sound behind me, "Blessed be the glory of the LORD in His place [above the expanse]." And then I heard the sound of the wings of the living beings as they touched one another and [I heard] the sound of the wheels beside them, a great rushing sound. So the Spirit lifted me up and took me away, and I went embittered [by the sins of Israel] in the rage of my spirit; and the hand of the LORD was strong on me.* Ezekiel 3:12-14, (AMP). We will never understand everything about the Holy Spirit. Our human understanding is limited. The prophet, Ezekiel, had some extraordinary encounters that were recorded in the book of Ezekiel. On one occasion, he was taken away, in a vision, into a place in God that a man can go only by the leading of the Holy Spirit. The experience Ezekiel had was beyond natural. Just as God revealed amazing things to Ezekiel in a vision, The Holy Spirit will give us insight about the things of God. Ezekiel learned about the future of the nations, revealed to him supernaturally. The Holy Spirit still speaks to us in visions today.

- We have access to the glory realm where God Himself is seated. *"Then the Spirit lifted me up and brought me into the inner court, and the glory of the LORD filled the temple.* " Ezekiel 43:5 (NIV). The Holy Spirit took Ezekiel to a place that was filled with God's glory. Perhaps it was heaven. When we are in God's presence, He will reveal His glory.

- We are encouraged. *"Then the church throughout Judea, Galilee and Samaria enjoyed a time of peace and was strengthened. Living in the fear of the Lord and encouraged by the Holy Spirit, it increased in numbers."* Acts 9:31 (NIV). Jesus told us we will have troubles in this world, but the Holy Spirit will strengthen us during those times.

WHAT IS GOD SAYING?

1. You don't have to wait to start a relationship with Jesus. You can decide right now. Ask God to enter your life as your Lord and Savior. Say this prayer; Dear God, I repent of my sins. Please forgive me. I ask You to come into my life and be my Lord. I give you, my life. In Jesus name. Amen. Write the date you made the decision.

2. Tell someone (a Christian and a follower of Christ) that you gave your life to God. Write that person's name.

3. Ask God to help you find a good church that is rooted in the Bible. Surround yourself with other believers. Write the names of possible churches as God directs you.

CHAPTER 11

GOD SPEAKS TO HIS PEOPLE

I remember when I was at a grocery store, searching for big clasp manila envelopes. I had a hard time finding them, so I looked around for an employee to assist me. The lady was very friendly. She patiently walked with me through the aisles. Suddenly, a thought came to mind: "Pray for her." As we continued to walk, my heart pounded faster. The thought was very intense. *"Could this be God telling me to pray for this woman?"*

Although I was familiar with how God speaks to me, I still had my doubts. I decided to take the risk. I asked her if I could pray for her healing (she was limping). She said it was okay but started telling me about several challenges she was facing. I gave her some words of encouragement and prayed with her in the middle of the aisle. She was very touched and could not believe we were praying at the grocery store. You see, I could have missed the opportunity to bless someone had I did not follow what I heard in my mind. I believe it was God who directed me.

According to the scripture, God communicates with us. He can do that in any way He chooses. He is a sovereign God. David declared, *"I will come and proclaim your mighty acts, Sovereign LORD; I will proclaim your righteous deeds, yours alone."* Psalm 71:16 (NIV). Let's look at ways God communicates with us throughout scriptures:

- God speaks to us in a visible form. *"Then the man and his wife heard the sound of the LORD God as he was walking in the garden in the cool of the day, and they hid from the LORD God among the trees of the garden. But the LORD God called to the man, "Where are you?"* Genesis 3:8-9 (NIV). God was looking for Adam and Eve after they disobeyed Him. Although the Bible does not describe how God looked, it seems that He appeared to them in some visible form.

- God speaks to us in an audible voice. *The boy Samuel ministered before the Lord under Eli. In those days the word of the LORD was rare; there were not many visions. One night Eli, whose eyes were becoming so weak that he could barely see, was lying down in his usual place. The lamp of God had not yet gone out, and Samuel was lying down in the house of the LORD, where the ark of God was. Then the LORD called Samuel. Samuel answered, "Here I am." And he ran to Eli and said, "Here I am; you called me." But Eli said, "I did not call; go back and lie down." So he went and lay down. Again the LORD called, "Samuel!" And Samuel got up and went to Eli and said, "Here I am; you called me." "My son," Eli said, "I did not call; go back and lie down." Now Samuel did not yet know the LORD: The word of the LORD had not yet been revealed to him. A third time the LORD called, "Samuel!" And Samuel got up and went to Eli and said, "Here I am; you called me." Then Eli realized that the LORD was calling the boy. So Eli told Samuel, "Go and lie down, and if he calls you, say, 'Speak, LORD, for your servant is listening.'" So Samuel went and lay down in his place. The LORD came and stood there, calling as at the other times, "Samuel! Samuel!" Then Samuel said, "Speak, for your servant is listening." Samuel 3:1-9 (NIV).* Samuel was a young boy about twelve years old. One night, he was sleeping, when he heard a Voice calling his name. He woke up and went to Eli (the priest), because he thought the prophet called him. By the third time, Eli realized that the Voice Samuel heard was the voice of the Lord. God communicated with Samuel in an audible voice.

- God Speaks to us through the Bible. *"All Scripture is God-breathed and is useful for teaching, rebuking, correcting and training in righteousness, so that the servant of God may be thoroughly equipped for every good work."* 2 Timothy 3:14-

16 (NIV). God speaks to us, encourages us, and corrects us through scripture. Every story has a lesson, a principle, or an instruction for our life. When we read scripture, it feels as if God is speaking to us about what we are going through. In addition, the words contained in the Bible have power. *For the word of God is living and active and full of power [making it operative, energizing, and effective]. It is sharper than any two-edged sword, penetrating as far as the division of the soul and spirit [the completeness of a person], and of both joints and marrow [the deepest parts of our nature], exposing and judging the very thoughts and intentions of the heart.* Hebrews 4:12 (AMP). Notice the words penetrating, exposing, and judging in this verse. These are action words. The Word of God is full of power. It is activated when we read it. Jesus knew how powerful the written word could be when read. In Luke, Chapter 4, Jesus was teaching in the synagogue. He read from the early writings of the prophet, Isaiah. Luke 4:20-21 (NIV) reads, *Then he rolled up the scroll, gave it back to the attendant and sat down. The eyes of everyone in the synagogue were fastened on him. He began by saying to them, "Today this scripture is fulfilled in your hearing."* Jesus quoted scripture on more than one occasion. In Luke, Chapter 4, Jesus used the Word when the devil tempted Him (three times), while He was in the desert. In each instance, Jesus responded with the written Word. He spoke to the devil saying, *"It is written."* Luke 4: 1-13. Jesus

conquered temptation with scripture to show us how we can overcome the works of the devil. When we speak scripture, we remind our enemy what God has already spoken. The apostle, Paul, reiterates how important scripture is to us, when he said: *"For everything that was written in the past was written to teach us, so that through the endurance taught in the Scriptures and the encouragement they provide we might have hope." Romans 15:4 (NIV).*

- God speaks to us through the Holy Spirit. *Jesus spoke to His disciples and crowds of thousands. He said, "For the Holy Spirit will teach you at that time what you should say." Luke 12:12 (NIV). For When David was hiding from Saul, some men came to offer support, including a man, named Amasai. The Holy Spirit came upon him. Then the Spirit came on Amasai, chief of the Thirty, and he said: "We are yours, David! We are with you, son of Jesse! Success, success to you, and success to those who help you, for your God will help you." So David received them and made them leaders of his raiding bands."* Chronicles 12:18 (NIV). The Holy Spirit will give us words to say, when it is time to speak. I believe, at times, the Holy Spirit will communicate with us, not only through our senses, but also in our minds (as an inner voice or a thought).

- God speaks through angelic beings. Hebrews 1:14 (NIV) tells us, *"Are not all angels ministering spirits sent to serve those who will inherit salvation?"* The heavenly creatures are real.

God created humankind, but also created the angels. Not only do angels minister to people, but they provide protection. (Psalm 91:11)

- o In Genesis 19, God sent two angels who rescued Lot and his family out of Sodom and Gomorrah, before the city was destroyed. They protected Lot and his family.
- o Throughout the Bible, we read about angels who were sent to deliver messages to people. Genesis 16:11; Numbers 22:35; Judges 6:12; Matthew 28:5, Luke 1:13, Luke 1:28; Acts 8:26.
- o God sent angels to carry out missions. Genesis 24:40; Exodus 14:19; Exodus 23:20; 2 Samuel 24:16; 2 Kings 19:35; Mark 1:13; Luke 22:43; Acts 5:19.

- God speaks to us through supernatural encounters. In Genesis, Chapter 3, Moses was caring for his father-in-law's sheep in the desert. He went to a mountain called Horeb. There, he saw a bush burning, but not being consumed. As he got closer, God called to him from the bush. Moses knew The Voice was God. Through that supernatural experience, God revealed to Moses his assignment and His plans to deliver Israel.
- God speaks to us through dreams and visions. Having dreams and visions is a phenomenon that not only happened in the Bible, but still occurs today. Joel foretold of coming visions and dreams when he said, *"And afterward, I will pour out my*

Spirit on all people. Your sons and daughters will prophesy, your old men will dream dreams, your young men will see visions. " Joel 2:28 (NIV). It was through a dream that an angel told Joseph Mary's baby was conceived by the Holy Spirit (Matthew 1:20). In Job 7:14, Job tells us that God speaks to people in dreams and visions. One of my favorite's stories is found in Genesis, Chapter 37. In a dream, God revealed to Joseph the future of a nation. Belshazzar, the King of Babylon, had visions (Daniel 7) and Peter had a vision about Paul. (Acts 9:12)

- God speaks to us through nature. He speaks through our natural word. When we look around, our surroundings speak of a greater being. (Romans 1:20)

- God speaks to us through human wisdom. God used people like the prophets and apostles, to speak to others. God used the prophet, Jeremiah, to speak against idolatry (Jeremiah 10:8), the prophet, Samuel, to rebuke King Saul (1 Samuel 13:13), and the apostle, Peter, to give a message to Cornelius (Acts 10:34-43).

If God still speaks to us, why do we struggle to hear His voice? There are things that affect our ability to hear from God and to identify His voice. Busyness, unbelief, physical and mental exhaustion, and lack of listening skills are some of the barriers that hinder us from hearing from the Lord. I will share four keys that will help us hear from God.

1. Find a quiet place with no distractions. Be still and quiet your thoughts. The Bible says, *"Be still and know I am God..."* Psalm 46:10 (NIV). Jesus told His disciples *"My sheep listen to my voice; I know them, and they follow me."* John 10:27 (NIV)

2. Focus on Jesus. Reading the Bible will help you know about God and His teachings.

3. Believe God is speaking to you. Often, we doubt because we think we are making things up. Many times, that is not the case. As we discussed in this chapter, God speaks to us through the Holy Spirit in a still small voice, pictures, mental impressions, and our thoughts (to mention a few) .

4. Write things down. Keeping a journal will help you remember and review what God has said. In Jeremiah 30:2 (NIV), God told Jeremiah *"This is what the LORD, the God of Israel, says: Write down for the record everything I have said to you."* It is important to keep documentation of God's words.

WHAT IS GOD SAYING?

1. Does God still speak to us today? Name ways He communicates with us.

2. Has the Lord ever spoken to you? If so, in what ways?

3. List one thing God has said to you.

CHAPTER 12

DO I WANT HEALING?

In Chapter 2, we discussed how God wants us to be whole and how we are also part of the healing process. Although He knows what we need, He wants us to reach out to Him. If God is all-knowing, why do we need to ask for help? Because He gave us freedom of choice. When we are in a relationship with God, we engage in a two-way communication process. By making our request known to God, we are stepping out of our comfort zone and looking up to Him for our ultimate healing. We can trust Him and believe He will do what He promises.

For several years, I worked with at-risk students and families within the school system. I would spend our first meetings identifying issues or challenges. Next, we brainstormed solutions and finally, we developed a plan of action. I remember situations when a client would not follow through with the plan. I could not understand why this happened. After all, the family recognized a need for change. Then, I realized motivation to change is not enough to bring transformation.

My approach to counseling is different now. I ask questions that would help me assess levels of commitment, before developing any plan of action. One way is by asking: "What needs to happen (steps) to help you recognize things are moving in the right direction?" Another way is to discuss the importance of their participation in the process. Their success depends more on their participation and actions.

I believe the same principle applies to our spiritual and emotional journey. Once we recognize our wounds, we can choose to do something about them. We can ask God to help us, as we continue to be involved in the process. Unfortunately, sometimes we hold onto our issues, instead of dealing with them due to denial or fear.

Living in fear will affect the inner healing process. Fear will paralyze us. Things become more difficult as we become used to our circumstances. We think things cannot change. At other times, we hold onto issues because we have a secret desire to stay the same way. We use our condition as an excuse to avoid work and responsibility.[xix] We would rather rationalize and justify our feelings and have others sympathized with us.

We might still want God to heal us, but we are not willing to be involved in the process. Jeremiah 29:11 says God has a plan for us to prosper, to give us a future, and a hope. What happens when we don't want God in our business? God has a plan for us, but He wants us to be part of that plan. Often, He is not going to do everything for us. It is not because He can't do it, but because He loves us so much that He wants to see us grow.

We tend to forget God's plan has its implications. While my salvation comes from Him, my spiritual growth comes from my active involvement in my relationship with Jesus. How many times do we not see a promise fulfilled in our lives because we did nothing about it? In James, Chapter 1, the apostle gives us some guidelines for life, such as going through trials, resisting temptations, and listening. Then he tells us we need to do what the Bible says

> *"Anyone who listens to the word but does not do what it says is like someone who looks at his face in a mirror and, after looking at himself, goes away and immediately forgets what he looks like. But whoever looks intently into the perfect law that gives freedom, and continues in it—not forgetting what they have heard, but doing it— they will be blessed in what they do."* James 1:23-24 (NIV).

In other words, we need to follow through with what God tells us to do. A plan is just a plan if there is no will, action, perseverance, and accountability to go along with it.

The Bible tells us about a man who needed physical healing. This man had a preconceived idea of how he wanted God to heal him. We read his story in 2 Kings, Chapter 5. The man's name was Naaman. He was an army commander for a King, named Aram. He was highly respected among his peers. Unfortunately, Naaman was sick. He had leprosy. In the Old Testament, a person with leprosy was typically isolated from others. Naaman's illness worsen and his wife became very concerned for his health. She wanted him to be healed. One day, his wife's maid suggested Naaman go to Israel and meet with a prophet, named Elisha, to obtain his healing. When Elisha heard that Naaman wrote a letter to the King of Israel, Elisha asked the King to send Naaman to where he was. When Naaman arrived at Elisha's door, he was greeted by a messenger who gave him instructions. The messenger told Naaman to wash himself seven times in the Jordan River.

Naaman was offended and angry because the Elisha did not deal with him directly. He did not like Elisha's response. In Naaman's mind, there were other rivers better than the Jordan River. Instead of doing what he was told, he complained about it. Naaman's servants seemed to have more sense than him. They talked with him and encouraged him not to look at the method, but rather the outcome. Eventually, Naaman decided to immerse himself in the Jordan River. He finally was healed.

The Word of God is so practical and full of principles. Many times, we think like Naaman when it comes to our inner healing. We know something needs to change, but we are not willing to submit to God's process. We need to understand that God is very personal. He already knows what we need. He created us. Psalm 139: 13-16 (NIV) says: *"For you created my inmost being; you knit me together in my mother's womb. I praise you because I am fearfully and wonderfully made; your works are wonderful, I know that full well. My frame was not hidden from you when I was made in the secret place, when I was woven together in the depths of the earth. Your eyes saw my unformed body; all the days ordained for me were written in your book before one of them came to be."*

Everything God does is good because He loves us. His timing and methods are perfect. When we look at Naaman's story, it seems that he did not want to be healed because of his own demands. He did not like the instructions Elisha gave him. In his mind, the prophet's directives did not make sense. Naaman thought he had a better idea. Thank God for responsible people that are willing to hold us accountable. In the end, Naaman realized that his healing was more important than the means.

In the same way, we are not spectators, but collaborators in the inner healing process. God gives us instructions and the grace we need to receive our healing. Isaiah 53:4-5 (AMP) tells us: *But [in fact] He has borne our griefs, and He has carried our sorrows And pains; Yet we [ignorantly] assumed that He was stricken, struck down by God and degraded and humiliated [by Him]. But He was*

wounded for our transgressions, He was crushed for our wickedness
[our sin, our injustice, our wrongdoing]; The punishment [required]
for our well-being fell on Him, And by His stripes (wounds) we are
healed. The healing that took place at the cross, when Jesus died for
us, is available to each of us.

God wants us to have an abundant life. John 10:10 (AMP)
reveals, *the thief comes only in order to steal and kill and destroy. I*
came that they may have and enjoy life, and have it in abundance (to
the full, till it overflows). Our Creator also cares for our mind, body,
and soul. In the NIV Bible, there are least 60 verses that speak to the
state of the mind. Approximately 40 verses address our thoughts or
God's opinions of a thought. Finally, God addresses the soul about
95 times. This is important because He tells us He took time to talk
about these areas. Paul says, in 1 Thessalonians 5:23 (NIV), *"May*
God himself, the God of peace, sanctify you through and through.
May your whole spirit, soul and body be kept blameless at the
coming of our Lord Jesus Christ." God will sanctify (purify, cleanse,
and redeem) each area of our lives.

In Genesis 2:7, God created Adam's body. He formed him
from the dust of the ground. Then, the Bible says that He breathed
into Adam's nostrils the "breath of life". Interestingly, the word
"breath of life" in Hebrew has the same meaning written in Genesis
1:2, where the Word *"the Spirit of God hovered over the waters."*
The spirit is connected to God while the soul is the house of our
feelings and emotions. Deuteronomy 6:4-6 (NIV) says, *"Hear, O*
Israel: The LORD our God, the LORD is one. Love the LORD your God

with all your heart and with all your soul and with all your strength. These commandments that I give you today are to be on your hearts." The Hebrew word for soul is **nap̄-šə-k̲ā**. It means life, self, person, desire, passion, or emotion. Sometimes the heart and the soul are used interchangeably, throughout the Bible. Perhaps God uses the word "soul" twice in this verse to emphasize the importance of loving God with everything we have.

God created us to function by processing sensory information through our physical bodies (sight, smell, sound, taste and touch). Then, our bodies produce an emotional response (feelings and emotions). As a result, we react to our emotions (behavior).

According to cognitive and neuropsychological theories, our minds contain the conscious and unconscious. The conscious mind is aware of what is going on in our lives, while the unconscious mind stores information with all sorts of significant material we are unaware of. Our thinking abilities, problem-solving capacities, and short-term memory are part of the conscious process, while our unconscious mind contains our long-term memory, intuition, creativity, spiritual connection, emotions, deep hurts, tendencies, and behavior patterns.

How can we access our unconscious mind to unfold past hurts? The Holy Spirit can move past hurts into our awareness (conscious mind) for healing. As I mentioned earlier, the Holy Spirit is the only One who can reach us at the point where our spirit and soul meet. There is nothing wrong with getting counseling, as I have said before, but our human ability can only go so far. God created us.

Ultimately, He is the one who really knows everything we need. John 14:6 (AMPC) says, *But the Comforter (Counselor, Helper, Intercessor, Advocate, Strengthener, Standby), the Holy Spirit, Whom the Father will send in my name [in my place, to represent me and act on my behalf], He will teach you all things. And He will cause you to recall (will remind you of, bring to your remembrance) everything I have told you.* " The Holy Spirit is the only one Who knows what is in our unconscious mind. He brings up issues into our awareness (through insight and revelation). Then, He helps us deal with the wounds of the heart. Many times, He does not focus on the 'why' but on the 'how'.

We also need to understand that once God reveals our emotional wounds to us, we are responsible for this information. There is no question God wants to heal us. The Bible says *"He heals the brokenhearted and binds up their wounds."* Psalm 147:3 (NIV).

THE INNER HEALING PROCESS

We don't know everything about how God heals our emotional wounds. As we established earlier, our human understanding of Him is limited, therefore, we don't have all the answers. Therefore, our first point of reference should always be scripture. While I carefully share the revelation the Holy Spirit gave me, I want to emphasize God's inner healing is not a formula. He is Sovereign and He will work in our lives according to His purpose for us. There are some Biblical principles that might assist us in our journey towards inner healing.

First, God relates to each one of us personally. He addresses our needs as unique individuals. God deals with us according to our personality traits, tendencies, and experiences. Throughout scripture, we have seen see how God dealt with each person. He contacted each differently. For example, we discussed previously how God met Elijah at his lowest point. Elijah was overwhelmed by fear, exhaustion, depression, and was suicidal. God showed up and healed him. We learned about Naaman, who was asked to do something for his healing. No matter what happens, we are connected to God as His children.

In John, Chapter 15, Jesus tells us He is the vine, and we are the branches. He also describes the love and joy that comes from being in Him. God enjoys our company. If you look at a tree, no branch or leaf is the same. Each branch has its' beauty. This is how God sees us. We are different and unique from one another. In John 15:15 (AMP), Jesus makes a transition; *"I do not call you servants any longer, for the servant does not know what his master is doing; but I have called you [My] friends, because I have revealed to you everything that I have heard from My Father."* Jesus changed His description of us from branches to friends. We are His friends. He also tells us that everything He does is connected to God's heart. As a friend, His heart is for us to be free, whole and full of joy.

Second, God's timing is always perfect. Sometimes, He heals us in the moment. For others, his healing comes over time. Either way, the end result will always bring freedom, deliverance, change, and transformation. God has a vision for us. Habakkuk 2:1-4 (AMP) illustrates this so well: *Then the L*ORD *answered me and said, "Write the vision and engrave it plainly on [clay] tablets So that the one who reads it will run. "For the vision is yet for the appointed [future] time it hurries toward the goal [of fulfillment]; it will not fail. Even though it delays, wait [patiently] for it, because it will certainly come; it will not delay. "Look at the proud one, His soul is not right within him, but the righteous will live by his faith [in the true God]."*

Third, God wants us to be involved in our healing. We must be willing to go through the process, whatever it looks like whether we encounter Him once, twice or more. In his book, <u>Doing Healing</u>, Alexander Vender says, "The primary way of healing emotions is to talk about them. When we disclose our feelings, we see what is behind them, and what we can do about them." [xx] If God requires us to do something, we need to get involved. He has already given us some advice through His Word. In Ephesians 4:31 (NIV), Paul tells us to *"Get rid of all bitterness, rage and anger, brawling and slander, along with every form of malice."* The verb "rid" means to relieve, clear, empty or be free of something. When God deals with us, there is always an exchange. When we give Him our fears, He gives us peace.

Lastly, we must take care of ourselves to stay free. We need to align our mind and body with God through:

1. Prayer. When we pray, we talk to God. We communicate our thankfulness, petitions, and needs. *Do not be anxious or worried about anything, but in everything*

[every circumstance and situation] by prayer and petition with thanksgiving, continue to make your [specific] requests known to God. Philippians 4:6 (AMP). When we pray, God answers our prayers (Mark 11:24). Prayer changes us at every level. Research shows that prayer decreases symptoms of depression and general distress.[xxi] Prayer also molds us into the likeness of Christ.[xxii] When we pray, we should also use our God-given prayer language (speaking in tongues). The Bible makes a few references to speaking in tongues. There have been theological debates about the nature of the languages (human language versus spiritual language). Still, the Bible records it. I believe the Holy Spirit communicates to God, through us, in unknown languages.

For years, I have studied the relationship between the brain and behavior. Science only confirms what God created and has established. A study, from the University of Pennsylvania Medical Center, examined the changes in the brain while five women spoke in tongues. They found that there were significant decreases in cerebral blood flow (CBF) in the prefrontal cortices.[xxiii] This is a breakthrough study. We know a lot of problem solving happens in the prefrontal lobe of the brain. I believe the Holy Spirit takes an active part in our decision making, especially when we pray in tongues. Another study found a negative correlation between speaking in tongues and neuroticism.[xxiv] In other words, people who practice speaking in tongues have better emotional stability.

2. Meditating on the Word of God. Meditating on scripture goes beyond memorization. We must think deeply about a passage or verse for long periods of time. If God healed you from depression, meditate on scriptures that talk about God's hope and joy. There is a reason God asks us to meditate on His Word. *This Book of the Law shall not depart from your mouth, but you shall read [and meditate on] it day and night, so that you may be careful to do [everything] in accordance with all that is written in it; for then you will make your way prosperous, and then you will be successful.* Joshua 1:8 (AMP). Remember, even Jesus constantly applied the Word of God. He taught us by example to rely on scripture.

    Meditating on scripture is not the same as positive thinking. Although positive thoughts help us feel good, it affects us at a superficial level. We need to deal with our thoughts through the truth of the living God found in scripture. We know scripture has a lasting effect in our conscious and unconscious mind. *"For the word of God is alive and active. Sharper than any double-edged sword, it penetrates even to dividing soul and spirit, joints and marrow; it judges the thoughts and attitudes of the heart."* Hebrews 4:12 (NIV). The Bible is our main reference for life. It gives us strategies on how to keep our mind and heart pure. Romans 8:5-6 (AMP) tells us, *for those who are living according to the flesh set their minds on the things of the flesh [which gratify the body], but those who are living according to the Spirit, [set their minds on] the things of the Spirit [His will and purpose]. Now the mind of the flesh is death [both now and forever—because it pursues sin]; but the mind of the Spirit is life and peace [the spiritual well-being that comes from walking with God—both now and forever].* When we meditate on scripture, we focus on what God is doing. Meditating on the Word of God also opens our minds to understanding. When Jesus rose from death, He went to His disciples. Jesus told them: *"Then he opened their minds so they could understand the Scriptures. He told them, "This is what is written: The Messiah will suffer and rise from the dead on the third day..."* Luke 24:4-46 (NIV). Here is an interesting fact. Meditating on the Word helps us in our problem-solving abilities and increases auditory attention (we become better listeners).[xxv]

3. Maintaining constant dialogue with the Holy Spirit. Recently, someone told me I carry the Holy Spirit like a dove over my head. Although I knew what she meant, I know it is the opposite. I do not carry the Holy Spirit. He carries me and He is very real in my life. He guides me, helps me with my decisions, gives me wisdom, and comforts me. The Holy spirit has spared my life on more

than one occasion. How can I not be grateful for His being in my life? When we stay in constant communication with the Holy Spirit, our life becomes easier to manage, *"You will keep in perfect peace those whose minds are steadfast, because they trust in you."* Isaiah 26:3 (NIV). In the book <u>Holy Spirit</u>, Benny Hinn encourages us to make a place for Him. He has equality among God and Jesus.[xxvi] We must honor Him, as well. The Holy Spirit will help us in our weaknesses (Romans 8:26).

4. Staying in fellowship with the saints (followers of Christ). It is important for us to be connected with people. God created us to have fellowship with Him and others. He created Eve to be Adam's company. God recognized it was not good for Adam to be alone. We are to *"encourage one another and build each other up, just as in fact you are doing."* 1 Thessalonians 5:11 (NIV). Find someone who has a relationship with Jesus and ask them to pray with you. Ask this person to help you stay accountable.

5. Build relationships with people who have a healthy lifestyle. As life happens, we might find ourselves in similar situations. Ask your accountability partner to pray and possibly meet. You can agree on a time or talk over the phone (weekly, biweekly, or monthly) until you feel free again. Also, you may want to talk to your leaders.

We need to surrender every area of our lives to God. This means we submit to God, while yielding any arguments, demands, or pressure to something else. This process will require us to give up something, even under pressure. It will take more than our will to do this. Hebrews chapter 12:1, says: *"…let us throw off everything that hinders…"* While Hebrews, Chapter 12, focuses on endurance, discipline, and the New Covenant we have in Jesus; it starts with a command to action. We must do our part in the process. This includes, but is not limited to, following the instructions of the Holy Spirit, meditating on the Word around a particular issue, or receiving someone's advice. Whatever the case may be, we are collaborators with God.

Because God has given us the ability to think and act on our own, we must make decisions. We must come to God and get over our pride and fear of man. *"Humble yourselves, therefore, under God's mighty hand, that he may lift you up in due time. Cast all your anxiety on him because he cares for you. Be alert and of sober mind. Your enemy the devil prowls around like a roaring lion looking for someone to devour. Resist him, standing firm in the faith, because you know that the family of believers throughout the world is undergoing the same kind of sufferings. And the God of all grace, who called you to his eternal glory in Christ, after you have suffered a little while, will himself restore you and make you strong, firm and steadfast."* 1 Peter 5:6-10 (NIV). Surrendering to the process will help us resist the darts that the devil sends our way. We can stay free.

WHAT IS GOD SAYING?

1. Where are you in your journey towards healing?

2. Identify which step(s) (meditating on the Word, constant dialogue with the Holy Spirit, and fellowship with the saints) you need to take to stay healthy.

3. Take action! Don't wait. Start right away and let the Holy Spirit work in your life. We all are a work in progress. The apostle, Paul, says *being confident of this that he who began a good work in you will carry it on to completion until the day of Christ Jesus* Philippians 1:6 (NIV). God is working with us and perfecting His work, so we can become more like Him.

NOTES

Chapter 1
WHAT IS INNER HEALING?

[i] LaBar, Kevin S. and LeDoux Joseph E., "Emotions and the Brain." in *An Overview* in Behavioral Neurology and Neuropsychology, edited by Todd E. Feinberg and Martha J. Farah. New York: The McGraw-Hill, 1997, 683.

[ii] American Psychiatric Association. *Diagnostic and Statistical Manual of Mental Health Disorders.* 4th ed. Washington DC, 2000.

[iii] Sandford, J. 1., and Sandford, P., *The transformation of the inner man.* Tulsa, OK: Victory House, 1982.

Chapter 2

WHY IS INNER HEALING NECESSARY?

[iv] Bayer, S., Altman, Joseph, A., Raymond, J., and Zhang, Z. (1993). Timetables of Neurogenesis in the Human Brain Based on Experimentally Determined Patterns in the Rat. *Neurotoxicology*, 14(1).

[v] Romens, SE., McDonald, J., Svaren, J., and Pollack, SD. (2015).

Associations between early life stress and gene methylation in children. *Child Development*, 86(1).

[vi] Johnston, T.D., and Edwards, L. (2002). Genes, Interactions, and the Development of Behavior. *Psychological Review,* 109(1).

[vii] Hendricks, L., Bore, S., Aslinia, D., and Morriss, G., (2013). The Effects of Anger on the Brain and Body. *National Forum Journal of Counseling and Addiction,* (2)1.

Chapter 3
HURT BY DECEPTION

[viii] Balswick, J.O. and Balswick, J.K., *The Family: A Christian Perspective on the Contemporary Home.* Grand Rapids, Michigan: Baker Book House Company, 1991.

[ix] Taibbi, R. *Doing Family Therapy.* New York, NY: The Guildford Press, 1996.

[x] Nichols, W.C. *Treating People in Families.* New York, NY: The Guildford Press, 1996.

Chapter 4
HURT BY A DYSTUNCTIONAL FAMILY

[xi] Zoccola, P.M., Figueroa, W.S., Rabideau, E.M., Woody, A.I. and Benencia, F. (2014). Differential effects of Poststressor Rumination and Distraction on Cortisol and C-reactive Protein. *Health*

Psychology. Dec 33(12):1606-9.

xii Morris J.S., Scott, S.K., and Dolana, R.J. (1999). Saying it with feeling: neural responses to emotional vocalizations. *Neuropsychologia,* 37, 1155-1163.

xiii Alia-Klein, N., Goldstein, R.Z., Tomasi, D., Zhang, L., Fagin-Jones, S., Telang, F., Wang, C.J., Fowler, J.S., and Volkow, N.D. (2007). What is in a Word? No versus Yes Differentially Engage the Lateral Orbiofrontal Cortex. *Emotion.* August 7(3), 649-659.

xiv Slavish, G.M. and Irwin, M. R. (2014). From Stress to Inflammation and Major Depressive Disorder: A Social Signal Transduction Theory of Depression. *Psychology Bulletin* 140(3), 774-815.

xv Biblegateway, https://www.biblegateway.com/keyword/

Chapter 7

HURT BY SHAME

xvi Zaslay, M.R. (1998). Shame-Related States of Mind in Psychotherapy. *Journal of Psychotherapy and Practice.* Spring; 7(2): 154–166.

xvii Gilbert, P. (2000). The Relationship of Shame, Social Anxiety and Depression: The Role of the Evaluation of Social Rank. *Clinical Psychology and Psychotherapy* 7, 174-189.

Chapter 8

[xviii] http://biblehub.com/text/john/21-1.htm

Chapter 11

GOD SPEAKS TO HIS PEOPLE

[xix] Pearson, Mark. *Christian Healing: a Practical and Comprehensive Guide.* Grand Rapids, Michigan. Baker Book House Company, 1995.

Chapter 12

[xx] Venter, Alexander. *Doing Healing: How to Minister God's Kingdom in the Power of the Spirit.* Cape Town, South Africa. Trinity Lidow. 2009, page 230.

[xxi] Al, A.I., Dundle, R.E., Peterson, C, and Bolling, S.F. (1998). The Role of Private Prayer in Psychological Recovery among Midlife and Aged Patients Following Cardiac Surgery. *Gerontologist* Oct 38(5) 591-601.

[xxii] Maxwell, John. *Partners in Prayers.* Nashvile, Tenessee: Thomas Nelson Inc. 1996.

[xxiii] Newberg, A., Wintering, N.A., Morgan, D., and Waldman, M. R. (2006). The Measurement of Regional Cerebral Blood Flow during Glossolalia: A Preliminary SPECT study. *Neuroimaging* 148, 67-71.

[xxiv] Francis, L., and Robbins, M. (2003). Personality and glossolalia: a study among male evangelical clergy. *Pastoral Psychology* 51, 5.

[xxv] Newberg, A., Pourdehnad, M., Alavi, A., and Aquili, E. (2003). Cerebral Blood Flow during Meditative Prayer: Preliminary Findings and Methodological Issues. *Perceptual and Motor Skills* 97, 625-630.

[xxvi] Hinn, B. *Good Morning Holy Spirit*. Nashville, Tennessee: Thomas Nelson Inc. 1990.

www.ingramcontent.com/pod-product-compliance
Lightning Source LLC
LaVergne TN
LVHW051245080426
835513LV00016B/1749